THE BAHÁ'Í TEACHINGS

The Bahá'í Teachings

A Resurgent Model of the Universe

by

B. Hoff Conow

GEORGE RONALD
OXFORD

GEORGE RONALD, Publisher
46 High Street, Kidlington, Oxford, OX5 2DN
© B. HOFF CONOW 1990
All Rights Reserved

The excerpts from *The Diary of Juliet Thompson*
in Chapter Eight are reproduced with the kind
permission of Kalimát Press.

British Library Cataloguing in Publication Data

Conow, B. Hoff
 The Bahai teachings : a resurgent model of the universe.
 1. Bahai doctrine
 I. Title
 297.93

ISBN 0–85398–297–X

Printed in Great Britain by
Billing & Sons Ltd, Worcester

Contents

CONTENTS

CONTENTS

Introduction

In the Bahá'í context, spiritual truth comes to mankind through the process of divine revelation flowing from God through His selected Channels. These Channels go by many names: we call Them Holy Revelators, Divine Teachers, Messengers and Manifestations of God, as well as our own personal Lords, Saviours and Redeemers. Although other ancient Revelations undoubtedly flowered in man's unrecorded past, the Bahá'í Faith recognizes the following historic religions as having been divinely revealed: Hinduism, Zoroastrianism, Judaism, Buddhism, Christianity, Islam, with the Bahá'í religion being the latest addition to this continuing spiritual progression.

God has never preferred any one of these religions over another, since He is the Author of all of them. Their purpose is twofold – in the general sense, the first is to educate and elevate humanity on every socio-cultural level, and the other is to provide specific guidance to the individual in order to bring about the full realization of every human potential. Each divinely-revealed religion provides a path to God that contains both 'inner' and 'outer' instructions that tell us how to reach His ideal purpose, that of knowing and loving Him, an authentic knowledge and love that in turn allows us to know ourselves, to love each other and to transform ourselves and society on every level.

Most scholars agree that history has provided us with many examples of spiritual ideational crossovers from East to West and back again, which supports the Bahá'í notion that truth must be accepted as truth no matter from where it comes. In the

1

Bahá'í religion there is a sophisticated conjoining of religious elements that can be considered Eastern to an Easterner, and Western to a Westerner, depending on the point of view. If we consider geography as a measuring stick, then we must admit that all the major religious systems have thus far arisen in that part of our world we call 'the East'. 'Abdu'l-Bahá put it this way:

> The Orient is the germinating place for the soul ... The Occident is the place of expansion. The West applies and solidifies that which the East suggests. It gives physical form and shape to the ideals of the East. But the breeze of God does not blow there. It must be engendered in the East.[1]

What 'Abdu'l-Bahá means by 'the breeze of God' is the return of the Holy Spirit from age to age.

It is not the purpose of this book to give the detail of the history of the Bahá'í religion nor to deal with information that can easily be found in any encyclopedia or library. However, it will be useful here to provide the reader with a brief historical background and some indication of the wide scope of topics its literature covers.

The beginnings of this new religion go back to the year 1844 in the city of Shíráz, Persia, where a young twenty-five-year-old merchant by the name of 'Alí-Muḥammad, descended from the line of Muḥammad, was singled out by God to prepare humanity for the dawn of a New Age. He took the name of El-Báb, Arabic for the Gate, the meaning of which has several significances. One of them is to signify the door or gateway into this new age, the Golden Age of a matured humanity. Thousands of Persians flocked to join Him, but both He and His followers were the objects of intense hatred by the powerful Muslim clergy. He was able to give His message for only six years, most of His teachings disseminated from the remote walled fortresses where He had been imprisoned. He was put to death by a regiment of 750 riflemen in the public square of Tabríz in 1850.

His short Dispensation stands partly in the old cycle, the cycle of prophecy and preparation, and partly in the new cycle, the age of fulfilment and establishment of the promised Kingdom of God on earth. Through this Gate, or the Báb, the believer must pass, symbolizing his 'death' from the 'old world' and his birth into the new. The Báb foretold the coming of 'Him Whom God shall make manifest' Who would follow Him in quick succession. This

2

'Promised One' would be the Architect of the New World Order, the establishment of which would be the same as the prophesied spiritual kingdom.

When a young nobleman and staunch follower of the Báb, Mírzá Ḥusayn 'Alí, announced that He was this 'One foreordained by God' in the year 1863 outside the city of Baghdád in Iraq, the majority of the Bábís, as they were called, accepted Him as their Lord. His new title, Bahá'u'lláh, which means 'the Glory of God' in Arabic, had been bestowed upon Him by the Báb before His martyrdom. Because Bahá'u'lláh had been born into an ancient family of nobility and wealth, the Muslim clergy, rather than killing Him for His acceptance of the Báb, stripped Him of His wealth, then exiled Him as a prisoner of the Ottoman Empire to Baghdád in 1852. Travelling with Him in all His exiles were His family, including His eldest son, 'Abbás Effendi, later known to the world as 'Abdu'l-Bahá.

Bahá'u'lláh was sent from one country to another, one city to another, always under guard, usually treated with great respect, even awe, but always subject to the capriciousness of His gaolers. From Iraq He journeyed to Constantinople, from there to Adrianople, and finally ended His journeys imprisoned in the fortress-city of 'Akká in Palestine in 1868.

His revelatory Writings fill almost one hundred volumes, most of which have survived to be published in some 700 languages and dialects throughout the world. Their subject-matter is all-inclusive and the literary style throughout is unique; it is both poetic and powerful, with hidden layers of meaning not apparent at first reading. Excerpts from some of His major Writings, as well as many quotations from 'Abdu'l-Bahá, have been used liberally in this book, not only to acquaint the general reader with the world's newest scripture but to state the fundamental Bahá'í argument or position on each topic.

During His Dispensation Bahá'u'lláh sent proclamations to many rulers of the world, some containing warnings as to what the future held for them and their countries, all of which proved true. He formulated the laws and ordinances that govern this latest revelation from God and outlined the administrative organization which would guide its institutions. Most important of all, He gave to humanity the pattern for the new world society which would culminate in a commonwealth of nations dedicated to preserving world peace. There is, of course, much more to this grand conceptualization of mankind as an organic, unified whole and its implications for humanity than has been presented here, an understanding of which the reader might wish to pursue on his own.

When Bahá'u'lláh died at the age of seventy-four in 1892, still a prisoner in Palestine, He left behind a following numbering in the hundreds of thousands scattered throughout the Middle and Near East. His Will and Testament named His eldest son, 'Abdu'l-Bahá, as the only interpreter of His Word and the perfect exemplar of His teachings.

Although 'Abdu'l-Bahá wrote few books, His words have come down to us in the authenticated translations of His numerous letters and the hundreds of talks, public lectures, interviews and audiences He gave when He travelled to Europe, the United States and Canada in 1911, 1912 and 1913.

Like His Father, He too underwent severe deprivations and suffering as a prisoner of the Ottoman Empire. He was finally freed when all political and religious prisoners were given amnesty by the Young Turks' Rebellion in 1908. Many Westerners met and wrote about this saintly but practical man who seemed wise and loving beyond description, and few went away unimpressed, whether ordinary and poor or politicians and clergy. He slept and ate little, spending most of His time between Haifa and 'Akká tending to the sick and the poor, administering the affairs of a world religion that was growing by leaps and bounds, and building proper entombments for the holy remains of the Báb on the slopes of Mount Carmel in Haifa and for Bahá'u'lláh near 'Akká. He carried on a voluminous correspondence and always seemed to find time to answer each letter personally. He had once remarked that even as a little boy He had grown old. World War I was a particularly trying time for 'Abdu'l-Bahá: the commander of the Turkish forces, Jamál Páshá, had threatened to torture and crucify Him, and His life was only saved at the last minute by the British army under General Allenby. In 1920 He was knighted by Great Britain for His humanitarian services to the people of Palestine during that war. 'Abdu'l-Bahá died in 1921, His loss mourned by Easterners and Westerners alike.

At the time of writing (1990) adherents of the Bahá'í Faith number about five and a half million throughout the world.

The reader will soon note that I have only selectively quoted or drawn from other religious or philosophic sources to support a point of view or reinforce a particular argument. This was not done out of any disrespect to either source of truth but only to show that a divine religion stands on its own ground of revealed Truth and need not be buttressed by any past or prevailing sectarian religious or philosophical thought. My intention is to present the Bahá'í teachings for their own sake. Religious scholars and students of philosophy will recognize some of the common threads of spiritual concepts that are shared by both systems, as well as teachings that are unique. Some ideas will be seen as restatements or a fresh treatment of age-old truths.

A three-fold purpose underlies this book. The first and obvious intention is to acquaint the serious general reader with a thorough and systematic presentation of the spiritual philosophy of the Bahá'í religion. Many of the academic texts and references currently in use contain erroneous material in matters of fact as well as information purporting to be the Bahá'í belief system. This book will help to correct those errors and clarify the Bahá'í position on the more profound spiritual questions facing religious philosophy.

I have refrained from using the words 'Bahá'í theology' since theology implies a growing body of interpretation of a religion's underlying philosophy by its central authorities and by individual scholars who determine its validity. Since Bahá'u'lláh's Writings are so inclusive, and 'Abdu'l-Bahá's interpretations and explanations of them so clearly stated, Bahá'í scholars are forbidden to change, delete or otherwise reinterpret their scriptures. Instead, they are encouraged to use their expertise to explain and expand upon the various spiritual and social Bahá'í threads of ideas and principles.

The second intention is to demonstrate the inevitable convergence of spiritual, scientific and philosophical thought whose truths are already uncovering the same shared reality bases. The unified model of the universe offered by the Bahá'í religion (which is also compatible with the framework offered by General System Theory) offers a powerful new design of reality and a renewed spiritual and social outlook on humanity's purpose and destiny which can bring together all man's endeavours.

The third intention, and perhaps the most personally satisfying, is to take the reader on a new spiritual journey that only the

Bahá'í philosophy can provide in quite the way that it does. The spiritual journey is old but the scenery is new.

I also wrestled with the current dilemma of whether or not to use genderless nouns and pronouns or to succumb to the sexually discriminating words 'he/man/mankind'. Since there is, as yet, no acceptable androgynous vocabulary, I decided to stay with the traditional terminology since it had to be used so frequently.

The metaphysical model of the universe this book presents is based solely upon the Bahá'í teachings and includes some inferences and speculations on my part which I feel are consistent with its basic philosophy. The Bahá'í point of view is presented logically, with the ideas in each chapter leading conceptually to the next, in journey-like fashion.

The Bahá'í religion teaches that spiritual knowledge is infinite, just as the universe is infinite. Also, no matter how much we may progress in the future, our inner and outer struggles will never be over. Without them we cannot grow or be challenged. There will always be another question emerging from the fuller explanation that grew out of a previous answer which in turn had toppled a cherished belief that long ago had been a problem that arose from an answer that . . .

Perhaps it is just as well that humanity's search for completeness and perfection leads more often than not to false clues and to wrong turnings; if it did not, we would never recognize Truth when we found it.

This book invites the reader to take this spiritual journey, one which will not rely on one's gullibility but on one's deepest desire to know and to understand oneself in relationship to God. It does not address an elitist crowd who see themselves as intellectually and spiritually superior. The ideal reader would be one willing to explore this spiritual path to God with no preconceived or traditional ideas about truth or reality, and with his accumulated intellectual, emotional and spiritual defences, biases and prejudices left behind. Only in this way can self-confrontation be followed by self-discovery, and self-discovery by self-transformation. And these steps constitute only the beginning, not the end, of the journey.

1

Escape to Reality

The worlds of God are in perfect harmony and correspondence one with another. Each world in this limitless universe is, as it were, a mirror reflecting the history and nature of all the rest. The physical universe is, likewise, in perfect correspondence with the spiritual or divine realm.[1]

Unity is the expression of the loving power of God and reflects the reality of Divinity . . . Throughout the universe the divine power is effulgent in endless images and pictures.[2]

. . . the senses are continually deceived, and we are unable to separate that which is reality from that which is not.[3]

Science is an effulgence of the Sun of Reality, the power of investigating and discovering the verities of the universe, the means by which man finds a pathway to God . . . Science is the first emanation from God toward man . . . In fact, science may be likened to a mirror wherein the infinite forms and images of existing things are revealed and reflected.[4]

. . . the function of language is to portray the mysteries and secrets of human hearts. The heart is like a box, and language the key. Only by using the key can we open the box and observe the gems it contains . . . The explanation of divine teachings can only be through this medium.[5]

Philosophy is of two kinds: natural and divine. Natural philosophy seeks knowledge of physical verities and explains material phenomena, whereas divine philosophy deals with ideal verities and phenomena of the spirit . . . divine philosophy – which has for its object the sublimation of human

7

nature, spiritual advancement, heavenly guidance for the development of the human race, attainment to the breaths of the Holy Spirit and knowledge of the verities of God – has been outdistanced and neglected . . .

We must discover for ourselves where and what reality is.[6]

A Planetary Fable

Let us suppose that on a planet in a far-off galaxy slowly rotating in one of the farthest and oldest sectors of our universe, a very old civilization has evolved. This planet has had billions of years to perfect itself and the beings who have arisen on it. Aeons ago they learned how to send information about themselves to solar systems containing intelligent life.

Our planet received and then deciphered these messages after much effort. We learned that those beings live out their lives much differently from ours. They undergo five highly specialized and distinct biological transformations each involving a hibernation from which they emerge quite different from before, much as our own *Lepidoptera* do. Each life cycle is like an evolutionary parade of their species' history, passing from a fish-like form during which cycle they live in a watery environment, to an amphibious form, and finally emerging in their last cycle as a humanoid. The individual retains no memory of its former transformations, just as we humans retain no memory of our nine-month cycle in our mother's womb.

This alien species' culture, history and knowledge are all contained in machines of varying complexity so that an individual can avail himself of information pertaining to the current level of his life-cycle or to any former life-cycle. Thus, he has knowledge and understanding of his own kind and his civilization on every level except those not yet experienced. Since he can never know his future, he has developed a lively and speculative literature and philosophy about it. He is always much amused by his previous speculations once he has been tranformed to his next level. This kind of life-spanning, as they refer to it, has produced a unified civilization that is philosophical and creative and a people possessing a great sense of humour.

Our scientists also learned that these individuals live to be 200 years old and have few diseases because their bodies regenerate after each life-cycle. The aliens ended their message by saying they wished to share and exchange knowledge with us and that they were able to teleport instantly anyone who wished to visit them and their planet.

A select group of scientists and politically important people were appointed as the first delegation from Earth to another planet. When the delegation arrived it observed that the planet was much smaller than Earth, with no moon, and although the large red sun cast a rosy glow, the members spent most of their time shivering. Our select group was met by that planet's welcoming committee consisting of their most respected 'fivers', a word roughly translated to mean those individuals in their last and most humanoid life-cycle. The group from Earth was surprised to discover that the aliens measured only about three feet in height or less, a fact which made our representatives immediately feel superior to them. Their bodies were thin and spindly, making them seem to be either on the verge of illness or death.

The aliens fortunately compensated for the greater height and weight (mass) of their guests by providing them with some cumbersome footwear, which caused much laughter on their part. Adding to our delegation's discomfort was the fact that this planet rotated in the opposite direction from Earth, giving everything a kind of 'left-handedness'. Our delegation was also perplexed by their hosts' habit of retiring inside their homes for a nap every three hours. When they emerged they began a prolonged nibbling at food amid much good-natured but accelerated cross-talk.

When our delegation asked the whereabouts of the life-forms from the first and middle cycles, it was told that the 'firsters' are mostly aquatic and are the equivalent of the human embryo. Although the parents love them very much, they are more like adorable and cuddly pets, their senses and minds only tenuously connected to their parents' world. When they reach the second cycle they are cared for and educated by special guardians. One of the fivers apologized for not being able to show their visitors the bounded cultures of the middle cycles.

They also expressed regret for not being more adept at our language and explained that communication solely by articulated phonemes tapered considerably in their last life-cycle.

'We communicate much more quickly and poetically and with

9

fewer misunderstandings by using thought-images. This is not telepathy but a communication shorthand which enables us to transmit blocks of pictured thoughts and ideas. As a result, we have become much more empathetic to the needs of others.'

Another fiver continued, 'We understand your world is divided into racial, religious and politico-economic strata which prevent you from taking time to reflect upon the nature of transiency and permanency in your lives. In our world the boundaries which separate us are based upon the natural differences created by our biological transitions. For example, our middle life-spanners know nothing about us, nor do they know you are here. They are farmers and builders and run our planet's commerce. In them, aggression and competition reach their zenith. In that life-cycle,' he concluded sadly, 'wars used to be waged.'

Yet another spoke, expanding this theme. 'We have experimented with every possible variety and combination of what you call competition and cooperation to order our lives. We have observed that every living thing evolves towards unity with its kind without loss of individual uniqueness. Our civilization has learned that peace and harmony become possible when competition is balanced with cooperation. Do you also agree with this?'

The exchange of information was a frustrating experience for our delegation. Our scientists had determined earlier that this alien planet took about ninety of our days to revolve about its dying sun and during that time it rotated only four times. Since darkness or nightfall occurred only four times a year, the humanoids had divided light-time into equivalents of six of our hours, dozing for three, and active for three. With this information came the realization that these benignly brilliant but diminutively frail creatures did not live 200 of our years, but 200 of *theirs*, equivalent roughly to fifty years of our time. Our scientists decided that while their civilization was undoubtedly very advanced and suited them very well, its philosophy and perception of reality was so alien that it would only confuse the human beings on Earth. After sixteen of their days, our delegation arrived back on Earth four days later.

After a few lengthy meetings between the delegation and major world leaders, our government released a short official report. It stated that our human species was physically superior to theirs and that in comparison our cultural level of development was 'equal but different'. The report also minimized the importance of any useful exchange of information with them in the future saying that their general philosophy of life was 'vague, ambiguous and impractical'. Governments promised to give the full report to special committees for further study. The various media named the aliens the 'Circadians' since they seemed to be obsessed with cycles. The only technology our government assigned a high priority to was their secret of instantaneous teleportation, which our physicists were never able to figure out. Other data was classified to prevent further shifts in the balance of power.

However, certain details of the mission were later published by one of the team's anthropologists who refused to sign all the agreements and waivers and was subsequently fired by his university. His version was categorically denied by all the other members of the delegation and his credibility was called into question. One of his statements lit a spark in the general populace which remained long after the official version ceased to be of general interest. He wrote that these humanoids believed in an Ultimate One Who Gives Meaning, equated with our concept of God. They had only one religion which they said 'was the disguise of the Eternal Meaning which each person had to penetrate'. These intriguing words were the only ones that people remembered and talked about and they caused a transformation of sorts in the life cycle of our own human species.

The above story fantasizes an other-galactic intelligent life-form evolving with a different reality containing different truths. If other realities and truths can shape our universe in ways other than what is familiar to us, how likely is it that we may have invented reality to suit ourselves on our own remote planet? Perhaps 'truth' is nothing more than civilization's fictionalized account of the universe. Is it possible to know anything for certain?

The Instincts of Seeking and Knowing

If we could state the fundamental motivations which underlie all human endeavours they might very well be our drives *to seek* and *to know*. Unlike our animal cousins who have in common with us the instinct of curiosity, the human being long ago learned the advantages of sharing what he sought and what he knew with others. Group knowledge led to directed group action and human culture was born. Culture is designed to eliminate problems but it also creates as many as it solves, both for society and for the individual. These problems arise because while the basic human rights of seeking and knowing are equal, unfortunately, we who pursue them are not.

What each of us seeks depends upon differing subjective scales of value, while unequal opportunities and capabilities for acquiring and processing knowledge have been thrust upon us in troublesome ways. In addition, each of us seems to be motivated by highly personalized incentives for what we want to learn. If 'we are what we know' then notions of reality fluctuate, engage and disengage from one person to another, one culture to another, even one world to another. Whose invention, exactly, is this shifting state of affairs we call reality?

We rely upon religion, philosophy and science to define reality for us. But each of these endeavours goes about this task using a different methodology, and only the one science uses is self-correcting. Philosophers seek truth and knowledge based upon conflicting statements of logical argument that they hope will 'prove' their own particular point of view. When religions become secularized their scholars redefine their Founders' teachings to accommodate the current trends and standards of truth. The hidden message of philosophy and secularized religion is that it is easier to reshape reality than to discover it.

If anyone seeks true knowledge of reality then he must prepare both for his own self-discipline and for a disciplined endeavour that will involve rules of logical consistency, individual dedication and capacity, many intellectual traps and, most of all, complete honesty on his part. For individuals who get caught up in this pursuit there is no other knowledge or reward more important. The problem is knowing when truth has been stumbled upon.

The Circle of Truth and Knowledge

Life teaches that knowledge exists on many levels, from the factual, concrete and practical to the imprecise, subjective, intuitive and abstract. In the first case we can usually see the results in some tangible way; in the second the results are seldom clear, often remaining in the world of ideas or theories. In both cases knowledge that has been previously authenticated as 'true' may later prove to contain incorrect or even worthless data. Much of what we think we know as certain and exact has undergone modifications and changes and may remain indefinitely incomplete, as Gödel's Theorem seems to prove. An old Muslim proverb might help us put the problem into perspective: *Knowledge is one point, which the foolish have multiplied.*

These imperfect and incomplete bases of knowledge form the intellectual foundations for the majority of the decisions we make throughout our lives, with feelings and emotions, intuition and insight filling in the blank areas. With such a large number of variables linking up in limitless combinations, is it any wonder that each one of us is not only a unique being but is also uniquely unable truly to understand anyone else?

Life also teaches us that truth is seldom what anybody thinks it is. It can be likened to the 'trickle down' theory which explains how wealth is spread to the masses: most of us get only a little of it. Truth also has many aspects, and like knowledge, remains forever one. Ideally, the object of learning should be the pursuit of that illusive point – truth. Whenever that goal is attained truth and knowledge merge to become one thing, one point.

But few of us have been trained to seek truth as scientists and philosophers. Most of us rely upon those trained in religious thought and literature to guide us to the 'truth'. Indeed, it is the world's religions which actively and even eagerly look for students to convert to their explanations of truth. Without disciplined instruction in that which all of these religions teach, we flock only to the particular religion our culture espouses and here we stake our own claim to truth.

What many discover is that there seem to be great disparities not only between the 'truth' taught by each religion and their many sects but even among the various schools of science and philosophy. Somewhere the path to truth still leads to the unification of knowledge. What we need is not just a new map but the *right* map to find it again.

The Bahá'í religion asks us to put the world's current paradigms 'on hold' and to examine a renewed way of looking at things. To experience religion is to experience a spiritual, intellectual and emotional journey. To begin it, we must start all over again, go back to square one and ask as if for the first time: what is truth? what is knowledge? The Bahá'í Faith offers a spiritual model of reality that is philosophically logical, scientifically accurate and spiritually unifying. Its teachings redefine real existence, the human spirit and the societies we struggle to perfect.

A Redefinition of Truth and Knowledge

Models require specific correlations and definitions, sometimes even providing their own language to portray a conceptual picture of reality. A model can be likened to a symbolic shorthand, a type of analogic thinking the fabled Circadians have long appreciated. Our sciences, particularly physics, have become especially adept in model-building and have set the standards for other disciplines.

In our model, for the sake of clarity, the words 'Truth', 'Knowledge' and 'Reality' will be capitalized to convey their usage as absolutes. When they are spelled with lower case letters they indicate their relative condition which is subject to modifications, changes and comparisons. Of course, from the point of view of God, such separations and differences are non-existent; trying to sort them out has always been our preoccupation, not His. The task of this book will be to show that the Bahá'í model is able to connect and tie together these floating abstractions into a logical and cohesive unity that will give us reasonable explanations of universal phenomena which at the same time translate into practical applications to life.

Our redefinitions begin with the startling statement that in and of itself truth, which we generally take to mean relative truth, has no existence except as a term of convenience. It can be defined as *our composite of those accurate statements we make about reality*. Because truth can be said to consist of *a collection of statements*, often preserved in writing, we discover that our notion of truth has resulted from how we use our language. Stated briefly, on both levels, Truth/truth verbalizes Reality/reality. Commonly-accepted 'statements of fact', however, do not describe Reality, nor oftentimes even observable reality, because their 'truth' is usually tentative and dependent upon other relative data that may be changed or modified at any given time. They are 'facts' so long as everybody agrees they are. The continued prevalence of one of humanity's oldest statements – 'the sun rises in the east every morning' – is the best example of this kind of 'fact'. Therefore, if we want to talk about Truth/truth our language must provide *accurate* statements about Reality/reality that remain permanently true. These accurate statements, in turn, become our body of true knowledge.

Put another way, true knowledge can be defined as *our personal and cultural accumulation of accurate truth-statements about Reality*, an accumulation that provides permanent substance and credibility. We will set aside, for the moment, the conundrum of just who or what sets up the criteria for determining what are truth statements and what are not.

A Question of Reality

At this point it seems clear that it is both culture's and the individual's perception of Reality/reality that is the crucial problem to be dealt with. These perceptions have been shaped by the ancient traditions of religion and philosophy, and more recently, by Western science. But when their perceptions of Reality/reality differ, or are contradictory, these dissonances create great rifts not only between these three traditions but also among the various individuals and cultures who espouse one or another view. Unfortunately, a shared and sympathetic discourse by their practitioners based upon a desire to unify these three conflicting frameworks has never seriously been undertaken.

The problems magnify when one of these three orientations to our world and the universe suddenly changes the content of its 'truth assumptions'. This has happened particularly in various fields of science which have bombarded us with so many discoveries and new technologies that their fluctuating model of Reality/reality has vitally changed humanity's vision of existence. But religious models have not changed accordingly, since their ecclesiastical institutions long ago invented their own versions of Truth/truth. The discipline of philosophy, on the other hand, has been reduced to a game of word-strategy and currently offers a model of no-Reality/reality. If there is a race for any kind of truth in progress, science has been in the lead.

It is difficult to believe that these three disciplines are related in kinship. We forget that science is a recent off-spring of philosophy; philosophy, in turn, issued from the intellectual fascination with the unexplored territories of knowledge that the ancient religions hinted at. The Bahá'í perspective finds no difficulty in accepting religion, philosophy and science as a continuing lineage of but one historic discipline – the discipline of revealing, studying and understanding Reality/reality, the 'ology' of the Unknown. Each of these endeavours has the capability to serve the other in an ideal checks-and-balances system that effectively eliminates the excesses and weaknesses of the other.

If the Bahá'í hypothesis is true – that mankind's first guidance to true knowledge came from special spiritual Educators, the Founders of our divine religions – then we can infer that their knowledge set the original criteria for stated Truth. Their explanations of Reality/reality were so unexpected and unusual that they often startled and upset their hearers. It was their divergent and thought-provoking views of man and the universe that gave philosophy and, later, science their original impetus. Unfortunately, religion's original 'point of truth' has since enlarged and multiplied to encompass almost any point of view that seems relevant or expedient.

If the Bahá'í religion claims to construct a new Reality/reality model of existence then it must make certain that it provides new insights when the basic questions of 'how', 'why' and 'what' are restated. If we admit to a world of the Absolute, we must show if it is separated from the world of the relative and conditioned, and how. If it is not, then we must present pantheistic evidence of the concurrence of the Absolute with the relative, and that they both occupy the same category, conceptually as well as materially. If this alternative is not acceptable, then our Bahá'í model must offer a better arrangement of the pattern of Reality/reality.

The difficulties to be overcome in achieving this goal seem insurmountable. The greatest hindrance has always been proof that an absolute Reality even exists. Mankind's knowledge of the Divine state is only caught in the glimpses that Divine Revelation has provided. These glimpses are further filtered through our own subjective and often distorted perceptions and understanding of how relative reality works. Western philosophy rejects a revelatory approach to knowledge, but the physicists who work with quantum mechanics are currently penetrating the barriers that separate the relative from the Absolute in their quest for one originating law, principle or force to explain our universe, and they seem to be paralleling many of the Bahá'í truth-statements. The mystical elements of true religion have persisted in telling us that behind the ordinary reality that we experience is an Absolute Reality which we have never seen but which offers perfect knowledge of itself to those who seek it, whether they be mystics or physicists.

The Relationship of Absolute Reality to Relative Reality

We will call the world of the Absolute the *exclusive* order since it excludes differentiation of either form or substance. By its very definition, nothing can exist separately within it, nothing is greater or superior to it, equal to it or lesser and inferior to it, as Saint Anselm postulated God many centuries ago. The Absolute must exist as a unity in its own essential oneness.

The second order can be called the *inclusive* order wherein all things exist relative to each other, are conditioned by each other and exist as a variety of ever-changing forms. We can know something of this last order, for we occupy it, but we can know nothing directly about the first, for that describes the world of God. If we cannot directly experience the world of God, how can we prove that such a world exists? And if it does exist, surely that would mean that God, existing in His Absoluteness, is eternally separated from His created world, the world of man. It would seem that the case would have to be one or the other, as the rigid logic of the Western mind-set of 'either/or' knowledge demands.

But an 'either/or' universe would not result in our familiar, relative universe. In a relative universe reality infiltrates all the spaces between 'either' and 'or', forcing us to conclude that all realities are not created equal. If all conditioned reality were equally relative (or equally real), the universe would exist in a state of eternal stasis. As the Circadian fable illustrates, reality has many guises, even though the physical laws which govern them are universally constant. That is, we are confident that the general view of the skies and landscape we see today outside our window will be the same tomorrow, next year and indefinitely.

We now know that relative reality is the 'effect' of the interaction of what we call space, time and matter, and that their apparent ability to shift configurations allow them to display varying aspects of themselves in the 'endless pictures and images' that 'Abdu'l-Bahá mentioned in the opening quotations of this chapter. As conscious beings we not only observe and delight in these endless pictures and images, we *are* the endless pictures and images!

The disquieting thought that we humans are able to experience only a relative reality in our own space/time dimensions through which our existences and experiences move, suggests that there are other scales, other orders and hierarchies of reality, perhaps all contained somehow within each other, yet open to our scrutiny. Our bewilderment arises from our mistaken belief that all of these worlds within worlds must behave according to our preconceived ideas of 'how things are' and are subject to strict human standards of verifiability.

It is this difficulty of certifying a methodology of logic to verify truth that allows us to translate 'Topeka is in Kansas' to 'Kansas is in Topeka'. Both premises are true, depending upon how we conceptualize the problem. It is precisely this subtlety that shows us how it is possible to make the ordinary logic of grammar work on one level of reality but not on another. But if we apply the logic of *conceptualization*, a logic which deals not so much with words and grammar as it does with linking logically-consistent concepts and ideas into patterns of wholeness, we would then have no trouble conceiving Kansas on more than one level, existing both as a state of matter as well as a state of mind. We could then say definitely that a small portion of the geographical state of Kansas exists in Topeka; and if the idea of Kansas includes a certain set of attitudes, a loyalty and pride of residence, then surely all those intangibles also reside in Topeka. Even mathematicians and physicists must at some point during the process of symbolizing truth, conceptualize their logic with equations.

Going from the particular to the general in logic is similar to going from the relative to the Absolute, for just as we can never know for certain when the 'greatest' or the 'last' generality has been reached, so we can never reach final knowledge of the Absolute. This dictum prevents any human endeavour devising an absolute method for verifying Truth. While we can stretch reality from its most scattererd and fragmented manifestations almost to reach the Godhead, that is as far as we can ever go. If

18

relative reality could ever become Absolute Reality, this universe would vanish.

The Bahá'í Model of Reality

Thus far, the Bahá'í model of Reality/reality is providing an elegant and reasonable framework for orienting ourselves to a universe that speaks to us both of the relative and the Absolute. 'Abdu'l-Bahá stated that the universe has been created for our education and that 'We must learn how to read the Universe; it is an open book.'[7]

Bahá'í philosophy postulates that the visible, material reality of our universe reflects the manifestations or effects of One Reality on many different levels. But how these multiple reflections are perceived depends upon which level each created thing occupies in the cosmic order of existence. Each level reflects only those particular aspects of space/time/matter which are dictated by the laws governing that level. As reasoning, rational beings, we observe creation from the constraints imposed upon us by our own hierarchic niche. If, for a moment, it were possible for all created objects to be sentient and allowed the gift of speech to communicate with one another, each view of reality observed by protons and electrons, stars and galaxies, flowers and forests, and by fishes and mammals would all conflict and cause such confusion that no understanding of the other's 'reality' would be possible.

Only the more inclusive reality observed in the unique level occupied by reasoning beings can be experienced and understood so as not to cause madness; for this scale contains not only all the characteristics of the gradients 'below' it, but also points to the invisible world of God 'above' and outside it. In the hidden world of Divine Reality conditioned matter, contingent space and suffused time have not been called into existence, and there are no statements or comparisons to be made.

Some religious philosophies have referred to these two worlds of Reality/reality variously as the Macrocosm and the Microcosm, the Greater World and the Lesser World, and the Divine Realm and the created realm. Our yearning for the Unknown to connect itself to us motivates all genuine religion, science, philosophy and great art. It is as though the world of Unity and

19

Oneness forever holds a mirror to our world and asks that we see ourselves in it; this is the true spiritual goal of the Sufi.

However, we should not make the mistake of thinking, as the ancient gnostics did, that Reality is a mirror that has broken into bits and pieces and that it is our task to gather the shards and fit them together like some cosmic jigsaw puzzle. Absolute Reality is not the sum of its reflections. Reality no more 'breaks up' than does the bent light in a prism, or the varying frequency-waves of the electro-magnetic spectrum. What we perceive in our Lesser World are the many facets of the undifferentiated Whole, but which we are prevented from seeing all at once. The Reality behind all realities remains forever hidden and un-detected, even as it encompasses the universe and gives all things their definition, shape and substance.

Also, we cannot see the shimmering and chimerical Divine Energy which sets real existence into motion and acts much like the push-pull effect that the ancient Greek philosopher Heraclitus called the *logos*, eternally merging and re-emerging into dimensionless infinity. In that eternal Realm all possibilities exist simultaneously as 'He doeth what He willeth'. There, probabilities, limitless in scope and range, either flash into existence or out of it, subject to the laws governing hierarchic order. Because we are dazzled by this hidden Realm of abstractions and possibilities, and frustrated because we cannot contain it, surround it or control it, we interpret its awesome manifestations in terms of conditioned reality. Those who lack vision see chaos and lawlessness, disorder and unintelligibility, and a universe ruled by chance and accident. How chaos becomes order, and randomness becomes structure with per-petual cyclic certainty, has yet to be explained by any branch of science.

When we look at the Bahá'í model we see that chaos and order are inherent in each other as a necessary and on-going process of creation, clues to deciphering the laws of our universe. They are but two perceived aspects of one thing, the primordial Divine Energy which endlessly creates and destroys universal phenom-ena according to the Divine Will. It is this Energy that connects God's World to this world. This idea was first intro-duced by Hinduism in its explanation of Shiva, the male/female god of creation and re-creation. If we learn to read the book of the universe correctly, it will tell us the story of creation which is the story of perpetual transformations and fluctuations on every level. Motion, created by the pairing of opposites – active/passive, positive/negative, chaos/order, etc. – in its turn makes possible the dynamic interplay of time, space and matter as they connect and weave their tapestries of layered realities.

The time has certainly come for the religious model, the scientific model and the philosophic model to recognize a common ground for truth and merge into one model describing Reality/reality. Truth can only be One Truth, even though its facets are infinite; certainly there is enough to go round. With the uncovering of Reality as its object, this enlarged model would reveal to us new knowledge about the obvious and about the hidden, thus expanding our clearing in the universe. The unadulterated teachings of the Founders of the revealed religions have laid the foundation for Truth and have shown us our place in the Divine scheme of things. Most important of all, they have unlocked the door to the world of the Absolute.

Bahá'u'lláh and His son 'Abdu'l-Bahá spoke of these matters without cease. In 1921 the distinguished and famous Swiss scientist, Dr Auguste Forel, wrote to 'Abdu'l-Bahá asking Him to elaborate on His position as to the spiritual proofs for the existence of God. The following excerpt is but a small portion of the Tablet, or letter, He wrote in answer:

> ... the mind proveth the existence of an unseen Reality that embraceth all beings, and that existeth and revealeth itself in all stages, the essence whereof is beyond the grasp of the mind.
>
> ... that universal Reality with all its qualities and attributes that we recount is holy and exalted above all minds and understandings. As we, however, reflect with broad minds upon this infinite universe, we observe that motion without a motive force, and an effect without a cause, are both impossible; that every being hath come to exist under numerous influences and continually undergoeth reaction. These influences too are formed under the action of still other influences ...
>
> Such process of causation goes on, and to maintain that this process goes on indefinitely is manifestly absurd ... such a chain of causation must of necessity lead eventually to Him who is the Ever-Living ... the Ultimate Cause. This Universal Reality cannot be sensed, it cannot be seen. It must be so of necessity, for it is All-Embracing, not circumscribed, and such attributes qualify the effect and not the cause.

... it will be made certain that every reality is but an essential requisite of other realities. Thus to connect and harmonize these diverse and infinite realities an all-unifying Power is necessary, that every part of existent being may in perfect order discharge its own function ...

It hath therefore been made evident and proved that interaction, cooperation, and inter-relation amongst beings are under the direction and will of a motive Power which is the origin, the motive force and the pivot of all interactions in the universe.[8]

The case for proving the link between causation and God has been revived by the Bahá'í Faith, and the next chapter explains how this can be established. It examines the Bahá'í concept of God and how it sets the stage for the creation of the universe.

2

The Originating Principle and Beyond

Know thou of a certainty that the Unseen can in no wise incarnate His Essence and reveal it unto men.[1]

So perfect and comprehensive is His creation that no mind nor heart, however keen or pure, can ever grasp the nature of the most insignificant of His creatures; much less fathom the mystery of Him Who is the Day Star of Truth, Who is the invisible and unknowable Essence. The conceptions of the devoutest of mystics, the attainments of the most accomplished amongst men, the highest praise which human tongue or pen can render are all the product of man's finite mind and are conditioned by its limitations ...

How bewildering to me, insignificant as I am, is the attempt to fathom the sacred depths of Thy knowledge! How futile my efforts to visualize the magnitude of the power inherent in Thine handiwork – the revelation of Thy creative power! How can mine eye which hath no faculty to perceive itself, claim to have discerned Thine Essence, and how can mine heart, already powerless to apprehend the significance of its own potentialities, pretend to have comprehended Thy nature? How can I claim to have known Thee, when the entire creation is bewildered by Thy mystery, and how can I confess not to have known Thee, when, lo, the whole universe proclaimeth Thy Presence and testifieth to thy Truth?[2]

The Problem of Definition

Literary attempts to articulate God and the Divine state are usually rendered by metaphysical metaphors and analogies or

23

mystical allegories. In the past, Western philosophy sought not to expound God but to prove or disprove His existence by manipulating the logic inherent in the rules of grammar, an artifice that often resulted in a kind of philosophical one-upmanship rather than truth. The logic of word-play works better at a disproof of the Divine rather than its validation because there is no sure method for 'proving' an unknown or unknowable abstract state or condition. As a result, the philosopher was forced to assume a set of 'givens' which one had to accept. This method was borrowed from the Greek practice for proving geometry's axiomatic assumptions but which only became the presumptions of philosophy. This semantic device neatly side-stepped the need to ascertain the truth of any 'given'. Few thought to challenge the unknown authority who gave all these 'givens'.

Ontological and teleological logical 'proofs' have now been substituted by one's own subjective reasons for a belief in God since there is no one who can prove another's personal experiences to be either right or wrong. The only other alternative is to accept a particular sectarian view of God as an article of unquestioned faith, and this alternative has always constituted the most dominant form of acceptance.

Still, if we can view all the above common arguments for God as sincere human attempts, then what they lack in certainty they more than make up in a nobility of intent. Perhaps all of them can be considered as possessing one of the many golden cords that lead to a belief in the Divine. It all depends upon what kind of validation it takes to convince or not to convince each individual, and which golden cord each prefers to grasp. With so many personalized preferences based upon each individual's subjective biases, it is not surprising that these differences cause most, if not all, the problems in accepting or not accepting one definition or 'proof' of God over another.

We now must ask if there is anything new the Bahá'í religion can add to making a case for God. In some four thousand years of recorded history our theological maturity has not progressed beyond the beauty and profundity of the Hindu *Gita*. In fact, it is now the theoretical physicist who seems to be asking anew these same fundamental questions about how the universe originated and how it sustains itself as it does, cautiously linking 'how' with 'why' and discovering that the fuller explanation may have something to do with 'Who'. The Bahá'í answer to the above questions, not surprisingly, is that there *is no separation of who–what–how–why*; all along we have been asking piecemeal concrete questions to understand *one* all-inclusive unified abstract process.

The Originating Principle

We begin with the evidence that all matter is born into visible existence from an origin that is itself neither visible nor material. We can name this powerful but unknown Something as the 'Originating Principle'. If we say this Originating Principle is nothing more than fluctuating energy, then we have conveniently erased the problem by calling it a 'given'. We must still account for how and why energy becomes radiant and from where *it* originates. If we say energy is the primordial force, then we are forced to conclude it must then act as the *effect* of something else, subject to its laws, as are all forces. Our next question, then, is to ask if the Originating Principle is actually the Originating Cause, and if so, can this Cause be something both intelligent and conscious? Would it have 'beingness'? Would it physically occupy the universe it created, or would it exist apart and outside it? Could it somehow exist as a part of us? Questions such as these take us in circles and, if we are honest, we admit we can make no further progress without help. We can settle for a type of vague deism, or give in to agnosticism, or we can tenaciously insist that if such a powerful, self-subsistent Originating Principle/Energy/Force/Cause does indeed exist, then explanations, if not answers, must also exist.

Studying the world's great religions would be a start in the right direction. The Bahá'í Faith repeatedly tells us that true knowledge of God can only come from the Divine Revelators who founded these religious systems. These first Teachers of humanity testified to an ultimate and all-wise Power who created the universe with purpose, and this all-encompassing truth underlies all other truths. Age by age, and little by little, They revealed the relationships and correspondences that exist between this Power we call God and the world of conditioned phenomena that is of His creation. Their teachings exposed the limitations of our own fantasized worlds of gods and realities and presented civilization with its first universal truths.

Historically, however, man has preferred to define God from the perspective of his own beginnings, his own experiences and his own geography; thus God more often resembles the cultural model which continually re-creates Him. 'Abdu'l-Bahá pointed out that, 'If we ever dare to limit and circumscribe God's purpose within any bounds, then of necessity we have dared to set limitations to the omnipotence of God. The created has dared to define his Creator!'[3]

When man misdirects his imagination even further, he persuades himself that each individual has the capacity to become God's chosen confidant, existing as His eyes and ears, His co-partner in the affairs of life. These people are convinced that without their human intercession on God's behalf, He is impotent. Such presumptions even transcend our attempts to define our Creator; instead the created have *become* the Creator! It seems there are as many fallacies of God-constructs as there are people.

> This people, all of them, have pictured a god in the realm of the mind, and worship that image which they have made for themselves. And yet that image is comprehended, the human mind being the comprehender thereof, and certainly the comprehender is greater than that which lieth within its grasp; for imagination is but the branch, while mind is the root; and certainly the root is greater than the branch. Consider then, how all the peoples of the world are bowing the knee to a fancy of their own contriving, how they have created a creator within their own minds, and they call it the Fashioner of all that is – whereas in truth it is but an illusion. Thus are the people worshipping only an error of perception.[4]

Since a creation assumes a creative power of some kind, to propose no-creator would also propose no-creation as a corollary. Most important of all, *any proper description of God must take into account God as the Source of all energy, whether potential or manifested.* It is this statement that becomes the foundation for all the subsequent Bahá'í arguments to validate a belief in the existence of God. For 'Something' to be able to create energy out of 'nothing' with all its infinite transformations, both material and non-material, culminating in individualized intelligent consciousness and identity-awareness, admits to a Creator with powers so transcendent and staggering that no one, not even the Holy Messengers, can fully comprehend power on that scale. Yet it is these Divine Manifestations Who have always pointed the way.

> Consequently, there is no pathway for man except the Holy Manifestations, for the Essence of Divinity is pure, is holy, and cannot be brought into the world of ideas. That which can be brought to ideation are the Holy and Divine Manifestations. Further than this, man has no other point for concentration; if he exceed that bound, it is an imagination.[5]

The Bahá'í Concept of God

At an informal gathering at a Bahá'í home in Washington DC on 10 November 1912, 'Abdu'l-Bahá was asked, 'What is the Reality of Divinity, or what do we understand by God?'[6] What followed was an explication that includes the most fundamental as well as the deepest meanings of Bahá'í philosophy. This argument, both logically and spiritually compelling, is one of the most complete arguments for the existence of God that has found its way into print. It is the forerunner of 'Abdu'l-Bahá's letter to Dr Forel with minor variances, this latter Tablet having been written some nine years later.

First, 'Abdu'l-Bahá calls our attention to the fact that, 'When we consider the world of existence, we find that the essential reality underlying any given phenomenon is unknown.'[7] We have learned to define things, not by their essential nature, but by their characteristics and by their behaviour. He reminds us that this does not mean there is no essential nature, but only that we cannot know it. If it is impossible to know the essential nature of anything, including ourselves, how can we presume to know the nature of a transcendent God? 'Abdu'l-Bahá says that we can make some assumptions about God based on what we perceive to be His 'traces and evidences'.

> That reality of divinity to be contained within human grasp would be after all possessed of an intellectual existence only; a mere intellectual concept with no extraneous existence; an image or a likeness which had come within the grasp of human mind or intellect. The mind of man would be transcendental thereto. How could it be then that an image which has only intellectual existence is the reality of divinity which is infinite? . . .

27

But the question may be asked, 'How shall we know God?' We know Him by His attributes. We know Him by His signs. We know Him by His names ... If we wish to come in touch with the reality of divinity, we do so by recognizing its phenomena, its attributes and traces which are widespread in the universe. All things in the world of phenomena are expressive of that one reality.[8]

He then describes the different levels of existence, those Kingdoms of God that express varying degrees of that Reality mandated by natural law. Nature is not another word for God, nor does God manifest Himself as Nature. Also, there is a great deal of difference in what it means to express, and what it means to manifest. (The differences are so significant and broad that this subject will be treated in the next chapter.) Divine or natural law, then, mandating God's Will throughout the universe, reveals itself as particular traits and characteristics in phenomenal existence that science observes and studies. When the scientist thinks he knows enough about how one of these attributes or signs consistently 'works' he calls it a scientific law, a truth symbolizing Reality.

'Abdu'l-Bahá goes on to remind us that all created phenomena must necessarily 'die' or decompose, for all things which exist are composed of atoms, and this law of decomposition or decay affects all temporal and finite existences.

Consequently, the conclusion is that life means composition and death spells decomposition. On this account the materialists are of the opinion that life is the mere conjoining of elemental substances into myriad forms and shapes. The materialist comes to the conclusion that life, in other words, means composition ... [and] the conclusion of the non-necessity of a composer, the non-necessity of a creator; for composition is all there is to it ...[9]

'Abdu'l-Bahá continues this remarkable exposition for the proof of the existence of a Creator by discussing various theories of how life and matter came to be. He argues that if we accept that life formed accidentally and without purpose, then what we see are elements that are moved by random forces outside themselves that somehow allow them to conjoin and sustain spontaneous cohesion that results in a universe of chance that

28

inexplicably directs itself towards remarkable structure and order. Aside from a lack of explanation as to why certain atoms will share their electrons only with certain other atoms, instead of random sharing, or why and how the accidental occurrence of this miraculous cohesion and orderly composition could occur in the first place, this hypothesis leaves us with only transient, short-lived, albeit 'perfect effects', that is, heterogeneous matter with no causation. 'Abdu'l-Bahá points out that when discussing the origins of the universe we cannot separate 'how' from 'why', nor effect from cause, because they are one process. For any theoretical science to look at only half the process (effect) does not seem to be in the spirit of true science.

'Abdu'l-Bahá next considers the origin of life as being completely involuntary, that is, atoms joining together because they possessed inherent qualities that attracted, or had an affinity for, each other, so that they would all involuntarily share their electrons equally and cohere with one another. This condition would produce a random but steady-state universe. With this explanation the atoms in the universe would be in permanent equilibrium; for atoms, once joined, would remain joined until all their energy was expended. Gravitation and the magnetic force, being constant, would forever hold them together. Even allowing for atomic decay, a bizarre effect would be the eventual coalescing of all gaseous matter in the universe into one cosmic lump! Heavy elements would not be able to form. In the case of these latter events, there would be no apparent cause and effect but only formless, gaseous matter joined in a finite, once-only, non-evolving dead universe.

Neither the case for an accidental conjoining of atoms nor an involuntary cohesion is tenable. What is left, concludes 'Abdu'l-Bahá, is composition effected by an eternal Intelligence and Power imparting the motive forces and energies which make distinct inorganic and organic existences possible.

Furthermore, it is quite evident that our kind of life, our form of existence is limited, and that the reality of all accidental phenomena is likewise limited. The very fact that the reality of phenomena is limited indicates that there must needs be an unlimited reality, for were there no unlimited or infinite reality in life, the finite being of objects would be inconceivable.[10]

29

God the Hidden and God the Creator

The all-powerful Energy in the universe is God's all-pervading Spirit. It has never ceased; it has always been and will always be. If we could imagine its cessation, it would be to imagine the cessation of this universe. Stop for a moment and try to imagine total oblivion. You make your mind 'go blank', but how can you imagine the contradiction of your own annihilation? When we think of 'nothing' we assume we are imagining total oblivion. The truth is, we cannot imagine total oblivion. What we do is to blank out conscious memory. Like the fictitious Circadians, the fact that we cannot consciously remember our previous life as an embryo, for example, does not mean this event never happened and so we can consign it to oblivion.

Perhaps we can go about this in another way. We will say that nothing but God exists and that He has withdrawn into His non-creating Essence of eternal silence where even the endlessness of space/time has ceased. If we try to fix a point, a picture or an image on which to focus our minds, we find very quickly that we are unable to do so. In one of His meditative prayers Bahá'u'lláh comes as close as it is possible to articulate this unimaginable state:

> I testify that Thou wast a hidden Treasure wrapped within Thine immemorial Being and an impenetrable Mystery enshrined in Thine own Essence.[11]

With this testimony Bahá'u'lláh presents us with an inviolate God Who needs no one either to witness or to confirm Him. In this aspect God is hidden, unknown, pre-existent, the uncaused Cause, and the pure and absolute Essence. All revealed religions inform us of this unknowable aspect of God which lies beyond words, beyond names, even beyond our thoughts.

> Wishing to reveal Thyself, Thou didst call into being the Greater and the Lesser Worlds, and didst choose Man above all Thy creatures, and didst make Him a sign of both of these worlds . . .[12]

> For men's apprehension of Thee is but the apprehension of Thine own creation; how can it reach up to Thee?[13]

Bahá'u'lláh reminds us that there is no accessible pathway or cross-over into God's hidden and eternal Realm available to us or even to the Holy Revelators. What we can seek knowledge of is God's 'Greater' or undifferentiated 'World of Oneness' wherein all created things have their origination; it is the World to which all things eventually return. It is as close to experiencing the Absolute as any created being can hope to attain.

The concept of God that is emerging points both to a hidden, veiled nature as well as to an evident nature. In the above quotation Bahá'u'lláh tells us that what we can know directly about God is what He has revealed about Himself in His creation. His handiwork, this universe, signals to us certain truths about energy and motion, about the composition of matter, and about the interplay of space and time. The universe exists, therefore God is. Within us and everywhere outside us, God's manifold evidences are evoked by His laws. This knowable aspect of God also suggests His consummate interest in what He has created.

We can also lay claim to know Him through the less obvious (to us) operation of His Mind or Will, His mercy and justice, and most of all, through His all-encompassing love. We say that God is near to us, that He is the Father of all, and, in both Bahá'u'lláh's and 'Abdu'l-Bahá's words, 'He is the prayer-hearing, prayer-answering God'. It is clearly not God's Self we see manifested in the universe or in us, broken up in some kind of pantheistic orchestration, but His signs, His reflections and His laws. God creates but is never part of the created. His Reality cannot be encompassed or contained, as much as we might wish it to be so. How can God have beginnings and endings?

Some people believe that the divinity of God had a beginning . . . With this principle they have limited the operation of the influences of God . . . if there was a time when God did not manifest His qualities, then there was no God, because the attributes of God presuppose the creation of phenomena. For example, by present consideration we say that God is the *creator*. Then there must always have been a creation – since the quality of creator cannot be limited to the moment when some man or men realize this attribute. The attributes that we discover one by one – these attributes themselves necessarily anticipated our discovery of them. Therefore, God has no beginning and no ending; nor is His creation limited ever as to degree. Limitations of time and degree pertain to things

31

created, never to creation as a whole. They pertain to the forms of things, not to their realities. The effulgence of God cannot be suspended. The sovereignty of God cannot be interrupted.

As long as the sovereignty of God is immemorial, therefore the creation of our world throughout infinity is presupposed.[14]

What 'Abdu'l-Bahá is saying here is that the creation of the universe is not an event in time, but that creation is always in a state of becoming; it is an eternal process without beginning and without ending. Creation, even if by this word we do not mean the creation of this particular universe, has always been, either as a visible reality or as a potential reality. The creational process cannot be limited necessarily to this current space/time universe, for it is quite possible that what we call our material universe has come and gone any number of times; it is the *process* of creation itself which is eternal.

In the following remarkable exposition 'Abdu'l-Bahá carries this idea even further:

The preexistence of God is the preexistence of essence, and . . . of time, and the phenomenality of contingency is essential and not temporal . . .[15]

The universe has never had a beginning. From the point of view of essence it transforms itself. God is eternal in essence and in time. He is His own existence and cause. This is why the material world is eternal in essence, for the power of God is eternal . . .

There are two kinds of eternities. There is an eternity of essence, that which is without first cause, and an eternity of time, that which has no beginning . . . Know of a certainty that every existing thing has a cause.[16]

The ideas contained in the above explanation are so thought-provoking and profound that they should be read again and again in order to grasp their significance. Some of those ideas will be explored as we consider a new way to view the begetting of a universe.

Bahá'í Cosmogony

The Bahá'í cosmogony is astonishing both in its profundity and in its simplicity. It tantalizes us with more than hints concerning universal genesis – it tells us more than we have ever known not

32

only about 'how', but also 'why'. It also informs us that in the attempts of science to answer with a definite 'when' our universe began, seemingly the easiest of the three questions to tackle, science inadvertently prevents any significant gains in answering the first two questions. In a beautiful passage Bahá'u'lláh simply eliminates the cosmic 'when' as having been improperly asked in the first place:

> A sprinkling from the unfathomed deep of His sovereign and all-pervasive Will hath, out of utter nothingness, called into being a creation which is infinite in its range and deathless in its duration ... The process of His creation hath had no beginning, and can have no end.[17]

Within God's pre-existent and hidden nature resides the undefinable 'somethingness' of all things in their unexpressed state, much like the unexpressed thoughts within us, not fully formed, but awaiting the proper time to be released, dependent upon our desire and volition. But what kind of 'nature' does an unexpressed thought have? Or, for that matter, one that has already been expressed? Here we struggle in vain in our attempt to describe 'essence' on a verbal level. All we can say is that this 'somethingness' exists in that hidden Divine Realm containing all creative possibilities. We come to understand that while all existent things have been released into a relative universe, they are at the same time potentially pre-existent in their origins and eternal in their essence with God. Their potential pre-existence, however, cannot be equated with the actual and essential pre-existence of God. In all the worlds of God the essence of all phenomena must have both an unrealized and a realized condition, otherwise that undefinable 'somethingness' of God could never find expression as creation on any level. Existence cannot derive from absolute non-existence, for 'the phenomenality of contingency is essential and not temporal'.[18] The Unrevealed is always waiting to be revealed, Reality always waits to choreograph itself, and the Causeless Cause is always giving birth to evidences, effects and signs. God, the 'hidden Treasure' and the 'impenetrable Mystery', is forever enveloped in both *what is* and *what is not*, and in His Divine Unity are contained the *yin* and *yang* matrix of all motion, all energy and all forces.

When we speak of God as 'the Reality behind all other realities' we are not speaking of His unfathomable, inaccessible aspect nor yet of His knowable creating aspect; this Source of all Reality is the living, dynamic relationship of God to Himself, the quintessential Divine nature where Reality never remains completely hidden, nor yet completely manifested, but pulses as God's eternal Energy verging upon recognition.

But *why* does God pass from His 'passive' nature into His 'active' nature? How does He translate His non-expression into His Word? Why should He choose to unleash His Power and create at all? Bahá'u'lláh answers in these three prose verses from His *Hidden Words*.

> O Son of Man!
> Veiled in My immemorial being and in the ancient eternity of My essence, I knew My love for thee; therefore I created thee, have engraved on thee Mine image and revealed to thee My beauty.

> O Son of Man!
> I loved thy creation, hence I created thee. Wherefore, do thou love Me, that I may name thy name and fill thy soul with the spirit of life.

> O Son of Man!
> My eternity is My creation, I have created it for thee.[19]

Certainly no human words can come closer than these to the intent of God as to His own explanation for creation. God's 'wish' or 'desire' to make Himself known is the conjoining of His Will (wish) and His love (desire), both aspects of His 'active' Self and from which He generates those forces that bring the universe into being. Viewed broadly, the relationship of the Knower to the known is identical with the relationship of the Creator to the created. Since we can step no closer to the precincts of God, we can only supplement this explanation with analogies from our human experiences.

For example, we honour and adulate great artists and thinkers by what they have produced and may yet produce. But what if these geniuses had chosen not to bring their creations from the world of thought into the world of production? If their desire was not to release their gifts into our sentient world, not only would humanity be the poorer, it would never have civilized itself. To continue this analogy, we know that it is possible for great ideas and works of art to exist in an unrealized state. When this is the case, then only the passive aspects of mind and knowledge are realized in this as yet potential 'creator'. He has not willed enough, he has not loved or desired enough, to bring substance from his inner subjective world into the outer world of objectivity. However, if he activates his passive self (we will discuss where this energy comes from in the following chapter), then he releases energies and inner powers that result in some kind of creative outcome. Although we have no trouble accepting this explanation on the human level, we seem reluctant to expand this notion to God, the progenitor of all creativity.

The Divine Connection

The Bahá'í spiritual map reorients the way in which we look at God, the universe and ourselves. It seems clear that creation exists within whatever boundaries have been decreed and desired by God, but that within these boundaries both possibilities and probabilities are infinite. Within these parameters all stages of existence reflect particular aspects of God's image with perfect correspondence. Yet, as human beings, we do not exist merely as a reflection, something not quite real or substantial. God's Spirit, or His Divine Energy, is the omnipresent force that, like an indestructible cord, ties us to Him and to His universe of matter, space and time, a continuing series of events all interconnected and intertwined in configurations that are orderly, stable, thematic and breathtakingly beautiful. To know something of these correspondences is to know something of ourselves; to know something of ourselves is to know something of God. God's greatest wish is to be known.

None of these realities are illusions or mere effects. Rather, it is our perceptions of them that are askew. We have not yet learned to see Reality in its non-visible range where there are no paradoxes. Little by little, the Holy Teachers have helped us to see this hidden aspect of Reality and to uncover the unseen patterns of true knowledge.

> . . . the Holy Lawgiver – unless he is aware of the realities of beings, will not comprehend the essential connection which proceeds from the realities of things, and he will certainly not be able to establish a religion conformable to the facts and

suited to the conditions ... Religion, then, is the necessary connection which emanates from the reality of things; and as the supreme Manifestations of God are aware of the mysteries of beings, therefore, They understand this essential connection, and by this knowledge establish the Law of God.[20]

This connection of the Holy Teachers with humanity is not only an observable historic fact in the form of the religions They bring us, but also exists inwardly as a spiritual state of mind and heart that allows the individual to personalize Their teachings as a subjective mystical experience. That such a divine connection is necessary in order to make God and Reality intelligible to us will be seen to be the pivot around which all true knowledge revolves. It is this connection that makes it possible for these Divine Manifestations to be the recipients of Divine knowledge and align our world with God's world.

3

The Worlds of God

That which hath been in existence had existed before, but not in the form thou seest today. The world of existence came into being through the heat generated from the interaction between the active force and that which is its recipient. These two are the same, yet they are different . . . Such as communicate the generating influence and such as receive its impact are indeed created through the irresistible Word of God which is the Cause of the entire creation, while all else besides His Word are but the creatures and the effects thereof . . . Verily, the Word of God is the cause which hath preceded the contingent world – a world which is adorned with the splendours of the Ancient of Days, yet is being renewed and regenerated at all times . . .

Look at the world and ponder a while upon it. It unveileth the book of its own self before thine eyes and revealeth that which the Pen of thy Lord, the Fashioner, the All-Informed, hath inscribed therein. It will acquaint thee with that which is within it and upon it and will give thee such clear explanations as to make thee independent of every eloquent expounder.

. . . Nature is God's Will and is its expression in and through the contingent world . . . It is endowed with a power whose reality men of learning fail to grasp . . . Say: This is an existence which knoweth no decay, and Nature itself is lost in bewilderment before its revelations, its compelling evidences and its effulgent glory which have encompassed the universe.[1]

A Spiritual Model of the Universe

Planet Earth is not the only home to intelligent, reasoning life in this universe. Both Bahá'u'lláh and 'Abdu'l-Bahá state that there are worlds without number where life is able to emerge, evolve and be nurtured, according to the elemental composition and conditions of each planet. They have also hinted that mankind need not remain Earthbound, but that, indeed, all creation waits to be discovered and to be known.

Further, They state that God has created the universe for the appreciation of the ideal, the perfected being. Appreciation is a quality of a knowing and loving creature, and can blossom into wonder, astonishment and awe in the spiritualized being who is striving to realize his fullest potentialities. As the gradual maturation of our own human race continues, this goal of ideal attainments becomes ever more achievable. As the culminating species on this planet, however, we still have much to learn and appreciate about our own spiritual and biological origins before we set out to explore other life forms on other planets. Both origins are irretrievably linked with the origins of the universe itself, in which physical and spiritual laws are not only intertwined, but appear to be one and the same. Our spiritual creational model of the universe, therefore, should yield new information about those beginnings.

Bahá'í philosophy is clear on the following three points: 1) the Divine Unity encompasses all things; 2) God alone should be realized as the one intelligent Power whose Energy, or Spirit, animates and dominates all things; and 3) creation is the expression of this energetic motion. Keeping in mind the Bahá'í concept of Reality/reality, we shall now see how the Bahá'í religion has put all of these ideas together to reveal an inclusive model of the universe that is unique.

Pantheism: The Universe as Manifestation

Before we begin enlarging the Bahá'í creational model, there is another spiritual cosmogony that we should first examine. This is the ancient philosophy that goes under the general heading of 'pantheism', which is the idea that God *is* the universe and that He manifests Himself in an infinite variety of forms, including ourselves. Its underlying argument is summed up in Aristotle's definition of pantheism as Real Existence being all things, but not any one of them. On the surface, this seems to be a reasonable thesis, for it would certainly explain the unity of existence. But it is also evident that this kind of thinking draws no distinction between God and His creation, God's knowledge and human knowledge, Divine Perfection and human perfection, and must logically end in the proposition that the Absolute and the relative occupy the same category and are in the same condition. One notable Western philosopher, Spinoza, had some problems extrapolating from this premise. If God and mankind shared Mind and omniscience as well as attributes, then all humans would naturally mature into perfectly wise and moral beings, with no exceptions. Spinoza accounts for this lack by suggesting that mankind was of a lesser manifestation of divinity but this still does not account for the endless differences and varieties of human characteristics and capacities and the obvious absence of any perfect beings.

The intellectual core of both Hindu and Sufi pantheism arose as the mystical response of followers who lived several generations removed from the Holy Teachers who had originally alluded in rather enigmatic terms to the veiled and hidden relationship of Absolute Reality to materialized reality, hinting that it is, yet it is not; that this is that; that all things exist in the Divine Unity; that all essence is from God, and so on. Mystics the world over have spent their lives attempting to unravel the meanings within meanings of words such as these to attain ultimate spiritual enlightenment. It is the final goal of the mystical search which is said to end in the merging of the human with the Divine, or the soul's 'attaining the Presence of God', a promise never before fully explained by the Founder of any revealed religion. Bahá'u'lláh wryly observed that although the mystical experience is not only real but is the fullest realization of the human soul in this life, it is the subject's interpretation of his experience that is at fault. After all, unless you are God, how can you ever know you are 'one with Him'? A mystical form of pantheism is no more acceptable or logical than its physical counterpart. For one to be true, so must the other.

The reason the pantheistic model persists is that it offers an egocentric explanation of the universe that allows man to share Divinity and causation with God. This kind of arrogance makes the Absolute and the relative, God and creation, a continuum, each merging into the other. God is the More and we are the less, with each having the possibility of becoming the other. We shall soon see that both sides of the equation are not equal.

True opposites can occur only in the world of creation, forming the continuum which allows for the possibility of their merging. But there is a great difference and separation between merging opposites such as active and passive, positive and negative, this and that, to form a unity and thus eliminating them, and merging the Absolute (God) with the relative (creation). The Absolute and the relative are not opposites and can never merge to become one.

Since the Absolute has no counterpart, God and His creation cannot be reduced to the same identical force or condition, otherwise that force or condition would be superior to God and would make created beings co-equal with Him. Thus, the basic argument of pantheism that God and His creation manifest the same realization and occupy the same category is both false and illusory.

The second argument against pantheistic morphology 'Abdu'l-Bahá directs to the difference between the *potential* pre-existence of created things and the *essential* pre-existence of God. The pre-existence of separate objects has only a *potential* reality. Specific and particular individuation has no pre-conceived nature, condition or identity; there is only the hidden Selfhood of God. To say that the relative co-exists simultaneously with the Absolute sharing its Oneness is a contradiction of terms. What is Absolute is absolute. The pre-existence of an as yet uncreated particular object has only the *possibility* of becoming actualized in the relative world.

'Abdu'l-Bahá's third argument discloses what might be called the pattern for the generating impulse of universal organization. (All three arguments may be found in 'Abdu'l-Bahá's discourse on pantheism and pre-existence in the book *Some Answered Questions*.) This final explanation summarizes all three arguments for the necessity of separating the Reality of the Creator from the reality of His creation:

> Briefly, with regard to this theory that all things exist by the Unity, all are agreed – that is to say, the philosophers and the Prophets. But there is a difference between them. The Prophets say, The Knowledge of God has no need of the existence of beings, but the knowledge of the creature needs the existence of things known; if the Knowledge of God had need of any other thing, then it would be the knowledge of the creature, and not that of God . . . the phenomenal is the source of imperfections,

and the Preexistent is the sum of perfections . . . So the pre-existence of the specification and of the individualization of beings, which are the things known of God the Most High does not exist; and these divine and perfect attributes are not so understood by the intelligence that we can decide if the Divine Knowledge has need of things known or not . . .

But the question of the Real Existence by which all things exist – that is to say, the reality of the Essence of Unity through which all creatures have come into the world – is admitted by everyone. The difference resides in that which the Ṣúfís say, 'The reality of things is the manifestation of the Real Unity.' But the Prophets say, 'it emanates from the Real Unity', and great is the difference between manifestation and emanation.[2]

Not only is the difference great between a universe in which God manifests Himself as in the pantheistic version of Reality/reality, and a universe which emanates from God, but the importance of understanding that difference is essential for any comprehension of revelatory beliefs. We notice also that 'Abdu'l-Bahá's opening sentence states that all things exist *by* the Unity, and not *in* the Unity, of God.

To explain simply the pantheistic version of a universe that manifests God, 'Abdu'l-Bahá uses two illustrations. The first pictures God as the seed which resolves itself into the tree with its branches, leaves and fruits, or creation. The second description is the more familiar Sufi metaphor of the Pre-existent Sea or Ocean (God) which manifests itself in the infinite forms of its waves, or creation. In both scenarios, God and the universe is One Thing sustained as the sum of its parts.

Revelation: The Universe as Emanation

To explain an emanated creation as taught by revelation, 'Abdu'l-Bahá compared the sun and its light to the connection between God and His creation. Although the light shines on all things, it is not the sun itself which descends and becomes it own light waves. He also draws the analogy between the speaker and his words, the artist and his painting, etc., to further clarify how the 'greater' can be separated from the 'lesser', and the 'knower' from the thing 'known', but still retain a very real connection.

. . . just as the discourse proceeds from the speaker and the writing from the writer – that is to say, the speaker himself does

41

not become the discourse, nor does the writer himself become the writing; no, rather they have the proceeding of emanation . . . The Real Speaker, the Essence of Unity, has always been in one condition which neither changes nor alters . . .

But the proceeding through manifestation (if by this is meant the divine appearance and not division into parts), we have said, is the proceeding and the appearance of the Holy Spirit and the Word, which is from God . . . The Spirit and the Word mean the divine perfections . . . The perfections of Christ are called the Word because all the beings are in the condition of letters, and one letter has not a complete meaning; while the perfections of Christ have the power of the word because a complete meaning can be inferred from a word . . .

And know that the proceeding of the Word and the Holy Spirit from God, which is the proceeding and appearance of manifestation, must not be understood to mean that the Reality of Divinity had been divided into parts, or multiplied, or that it had descended from the exaltation of holiness and purity. God forbid![3]

The World of Revelation and Spirit

Bahá'u'lláh reminds us that there is another abstract 'world' that serves as the connection between our materialized world and the unseen world of God. We are all familiar with that 'middle world' although most of us have lost touch with it. It is God's revealed but invisible world of His First Emanation, the world of the Holy Spirit. Because previous descriptions of this world were so obscured by mystical and pseudo-mystical interpretations, it has come down to us in such a variety of guises that many no longer recognize it or even take it as a serious spiritual concept.

The Bahá'í teachings explain that it is through this world, described as the primary emanation from God, that the souls of being receive their dependence upon God. It is this in-between world that gives us our understanding of how 'emanation' becomes 'manifestation'.

The word 'manifestation' also has another meaning in Bahá'í scripture. Bahá'u'lláh referred to all the Divine Teachers as Holy Manifestations of God. He did not mean that God Himself had corporeally taken on human form or substance; rather, that God grants certain divine powers and perfections to be manifested equally in each chosen Revelator. Bahá'u'lláh also reminds us that even empowered with these divine characteristics, the distance between God and these Holy Manifestations is greater than the distance between each of them and each of us. The rarefied world of revelation is humanity's link with God's Realm – in fact, our only link. Revealed Truth is God's way to Himself.

The reality of revelation is grounded in this world of God's First Emanation which Judeo–Christian–Islamic religions have equated with the Holy Spirit. Bahá'u'lláh has brought this spiritual world back to humanity with startling consequences; not only does it change our view of religion and ourselves, but it shows us the very heart-beat of the cosmos itself.

The Divine Spirit of God

'To emanate' means to diffuse or issue from an energy source. Universal creation emanates from God as His Primal Energy or Will, ceaseless in its movement and motion. It is the originating Power of all powers, the unified Force of all forces, and the first energized expression of God. Heraclitus named it the *logos*, Philo called it 'the Word', Krishna referred to it as 'the streaming forth of Brahma'. It is the Kabbalistic unity of the Jewish *Sefiroth*, the Holy Spirit first named by Zarathustra and so called by the Holy Prophets of God who came after Him. Both Bahá'u'lláh and 'Abdu'l-Bahá make use of all of the above descriptions to bring this Divine Energy into human range. In one place 'Abdu'l-Bahá states unequivocally that 'the greatest power in the realm and range of human existence is Spirit – the Divine Breath which animates and pervades all things. It is manifested throughout creation in different degrees or kingdoms.'[4] So elevated is the concept of this powerful all-pervading Spirit of God that to comprehend it is to comprehend the universe itself. How all created things can merge into endless transformations of themselves in an infinite universe is to understand what true pantheism means – a creation wherein all things are unified and where the germ of existence is one Energy, one Power.

Therefore the origin and outcome of phenomena is verily the omnipresent God for the reality of all phenomenal existence is through Him. There is neither reality nor the manifestation of reality without the instrumentality of God. Existence is realized and possible through the bounty of God, just as the ray or flame emanating from this lamp is realized through the bounty of the lamp from which it originates. Even so all phenomena are realized through the divine bounty, and the explanation of true pantheistic statement and principle is that the phenomena of the universe find realization through the one power animating and dominating all things; and all things are but manifestations of its energy and bounty.[5]

Manifestation becomes emanation's object, its recipient and its goal. But what is manifested is Reality, not God, and this Reality expresses God's immanent design throughout creation, enfolding within every essence its meaning and its purpose. Each and every atom 'knows' exactly what it can and cannot do, what it might or might not be, simultaneously exhibiting both its tendencies *to be* and *to do*. Even as it exists in its probability state, it is at the same time verging on actualizing itself as part of a specified phenomenon. But how can energy 'know' what to do or be?

If this First Emanation from God is the expression of His Will/Mind and His Love/Desire, then energy, too, must be both loving and mindful as it carries God's divine code throughout the cosmos. It is all a matter of how we choose to define this Divine Energy. Without its universality, God's speech could never be heard, for there would be no creation to hear it. We can go even further than this: *it is this animating Spirit of God that becomes the religious or spiritual explanation behind all creation.* Its power both surrounds and is contained within all phenomena. Through it, each degree of existence receives its essential nature, culminating in the human spirit or human soul. Everything in the universe pulsates and has its being through this agency of Divine Power.

The Holy Spirit

While this First Emanation pervades and sustains creation as a whole, there is another, closer outpouring of this same diffusion that personifies itself as the Holy Spirit to conscious life anywhere in the universe that has been intellectually and spiritually awakened. Through this immanent and direct outpouring from God, He makes Himself and His wishes known to us through the process we call revelation. Ultimately the power of God manifests itself for the benefit of the particular, the created being. Since the Holy Spirit is a more concentrated focus of God's universal Energy, it serves as His timeless 'open channel' to humankind. Were it to be removed even for an instant, the human species would be reduced to just another species in the animal kingdom competing with other primates.

But no particularized creature is able to receive this fuller surge of Divine Power/Energy. It must be 'stepped-down', much as a transformer works for a prime generator to give illumination to a single light bulb. A pre-selected lineage readies a special human being to be the channel for this Power. Each Messenger of God is prepared to receive a fuller and greater portion of God's Divine Spirit than has been apportioned to each of us. It is as if each Messenger had stood at the centre of a spiritual nuclear blast and come away with superhuman wisdom and love. With this one act, repeated over and over at set intervals in human history, the ordinary in us and around us is forever transmuted into the extraordinary. To believe that this divine event has occurred but once in the millions of years of our species' history is to degrade the omnipotence of God.

Bahá'u'lláh sometimes compared each Manifestation of God to a brilliant lamp through which shone the light of God. He said humanity then became attached to the lamp instead of its light. Although each lamp may appear different to us, the light which streams from them is one and the same. The mission of every Manifestation of God is to educate and train the souls of humankind so that they may reflect clearly the light and love God directs to them by means of these special lamps, so that each soul can be trained to truly reflect God's image. This is the story of spiritual illumination, rebirth and transformation.

'Abdu'l-Bahá tells us how this reflected Divine Energy/Power that is available to us is to be used:

> The Holy Spirit it is which, through the mediation of the Prophets of God, teaches spiritual virtues to man and enables him to attain Eternal Life.
>
> All these blessings are brought to man by the Holy Spirit; therefore we can understand that the Holy Spirit is the Intermediary between the Creator and the created. The light and heat of the sun cause the earth to be fruitful, and create

life in all things that grow; and the Holy Spirit quickens the souls of men.[6]

What is religious salvation but the freeing and educating of our darkened selves?

The Purpose of Revelation

Spiritual rebirth, or the transformation of self, occurs so seldom that most of us do not really understand what it means. It is certain that man's evolutionary survival traits were not developed as a contest to see how selfish, cruel and greedy he could be, but to sharpen those 'seeking and knowing' abilities and to temper them with a third instinct, also shared with the animal kingdom, that of nurturing. When nurturing behaviour expands from the instinctual level to the feeling/knowing level it expresses itself as love. All our animal traits have the capability to transcend themselves to the human level. Unfortunately, it seems to be easier for us to express these traits in their more primitive modes, perhaps for the reason that we have carried them with us so long that their gratifications have become expected, immediate and habitual.

If we consider materialism as the ubiquitous philosophy of life that has always been with us, we may discover that it influences each one of us far more than we think. 'Abdu'l-Bahá left us the following somewhat amusing description of a latter-day materialist:

All the animals are materialists. They are deniers of God and without realization of a transcendent power in the universe. They have no knowledge of the divine prophets and holy books; mere captives of nature and the sense world. In reality they are like the great philosophers of this day who are not in touch with God and the Holy Spirit . . . The animal lives this kind of life blissfully and untroubled whereas the material philosophers labour and study for ten or twenty years in schools and colleges, denying God, the Holy Spirit and divine inspirations. The animal is even a greater philosopher, for it attains the ability to do this without labour and study. For instance, the cow denies God and the Holy Spirit, knows nothing of divine inspirations, heavenly bounties or spiritual emotions and is a stranger to the world of hearts. Like the philosophers, the cow is a captive of nature and knows nothing beyond the range of the senses. The philosophers however glory in this, saying, 'We are not captives of superstitions; we have implicit faith in the impressions of the senses and know nothing beyond the realm of nature which contains and covers everything.' But the cow, without study or proficiency in the sciences, modestly and quietly views life from the same standpoint, living in harmony with nature's laws in the utmost dignity and nobility.[7]

The pivotal teaching of God through His Messengers is the reality of the human being as a spiritual creation. If this proposition is accepted, then it is not difficult to see how the non-visible worlds of God are connected to the visible world of creation through the agency of the Holy Spirit, a proposition which centralizes the three major points made at the beginning of this chapter. Now we can understand how the Unity of God can encompass all things without materializing itself as all things. It is God's emanation as Divine Energy and Power, His all-pervading Spirit, which animates and gives definition and life to the universe. The world of creation is a processional manifestation of that divine emanating motion, a process that has neither beginning nor ending.

As spiritual creations, we human beings have the capability of attaining all the grades of perfection as our birthright. But *how* this can be accomplished has not been made easy.

The world's religious books have told us about a nebulosity we have named the soul whose purpose it is to put us in touch with spiritual realities. For thousands of years philosophers have speculated on its existence and attributes. There have been many assumptions but few definitions. The main obstacle has always been a believable 'proof' that would not negate any known law of the universe.

Will our Bahá'í model break down at this point, or can it offer a clarification of such an unclear concept? We have said that any model must provide specific definitions if it is to remain believable. To do this, the Bahá'í explanation of the soul must begin at the beginning and speak of the origin of the universe itself. We will discover that natural and spiritual genesis are not two events, but one event. Before we define the soul, we must first show how all inorganic and organic life intersects with the spiritual nature of man.

47

4

The Journey of the Atom

Consider the aim of creation: is it possible that all is created to evolve and develop through countless ages with this small goal in view – a few years of a man's life on earth? Is it not unthinkable that this should be the final aim of existence?

The mineral evolves till it is absorbed in the life of the plant, the plant progresses till finally it loses its life in that of the animal; the animal, in its turn, forming part of the food of man, is absorbed into human life.

Thus, man is shown to be the sum of all creation, the superior of all created beings, the goal to which countless ages of existence have progressed.

At best, man spends four-score years and ten in this world – a short time indeed![1]

The Great Chain of Being

Of all the philosophical ideas 'Abdu'l-Bahá presented to His Western audience, few were more relentlessly repeated than 'the journey of the atom'. 'Abdu'l-Bahá had no training in physics, classical or current, nor was He presenting a science of physics. Elaborating upon Aristotle's progression of 'the Great Chain of Being', He explored the spiritual implications of the atom with its indestructible heart and how it began the ceaseless process of cosmological order and progression. The 'first' of all created things also becomes the 'last' of all created things as 'Abdu'l-Bahá uplifts the invisible atom as the carrier of the Divine Energy/Force which resounds throughout the universe, connecting and reconnecting to form particular patterns and shapes and functions all interrelated by their common origin. It is not likely that the majority of 'Abdu'l-Bahá's Western audience were able to set Aristotle as a reference point, as educated Muslims would be certain to do, and perhaps it did not matter. It was the idea itself that provoked thought, particularly since it seemed to preface or be included in almost every talk He gave, so the Westerner grew familiar with its renovated structure. Of all the Western philosophers, it was Aristotle who had the most profound effect upon classical Islamic as well as European medieval philosophy. In the Bahá'í model there are, of course, departures from Aristotle's scheme, both general and particular, based as it is upon the revelatory propositions of Bahá'u'lláh.

This idea of following the atom through the hierarchy of real existence to show how all phenomena are interrelated and interconnected is the basic dominant thought that runs throughout Bahá'í philosophy. As the Bahá'í explanation of created phenomena it must be understood before any other major theme can be introduced.

The Hierarchy of God's Creation

Our first chapter established Reality as presenting itself to us in degrees or gradients, and although Reality is one, it is our observation and perception of it that limits our interpretation of it. All things in our universe occupy one of these special niches and are bound by laws. One of these laws prohibits any occupant of one level 'jumping' to another. Another law of progressive existence specifies that each order will carry within it all the features from the gradients 'below' it as well as those features unique to it. A corollary to this law is that no occupant of any level can know for certain the features of the degrees 'above' it, similar to the fictional Circadians' experiences of their life cycles.

These kingdoms of creation were named by Aristotle the 'mineral kingdom', the 'plant kingdom', the 'animal kingdom' and the 'human kingdom'. This nomenclature still stands. The author has added one more – the 'nuclear kingdom' – to complete the chain. Each of these levels displays a particular evolution of matter, its particular population manifesting both identifiable physical and spiritual limits as its hallmark of the universal and Divine Energy/Spirit.

The elemental atoms which constitute all phenomenal existence and being in this illimitable universe are in perpetual motion, undergoing continuous degrees of progression . . . for after disintegration of the human body into which it has entered, it returns to the mineral kingdom whence it came, and will continue to traverse the kingdoms of phenomena as before . . .

In its ceaseless progression and journeyings the atom becomes imbued with the virtues and powers of each degree or kingdom it traverses. In the degree of the mineral it possessed mineral affinities; in the kingdom of the vegetable it manifested the virtue augmentative or power of growth; in the animal organism it reflected the intelligence of that degree, and in the kingdom of man it was qualified with human attributes or virtues . . . No atom is bereft or deprived of this opportunity or right of expression. Nor can it be said of any given atom that it is denied equal opportunities with other atoms; nay, all are privileged to possess the virtues existent in these kingdoms and to reflect the attributes of their organisms.[2]

This long forgotten philosophical idea, revived once more by the Bahá'í religion, contains several other thought-provoking ideas in this holistic model of unified matter. It sees the lowly but sublime atom almost as eternal as God's Divine Spirit, that pure primordial energy which pervades the universe without cessation. If this is true, then it would appear that energy is always in a process of being created. Bahá'u'lláh affirms that God's Spirit/Energy continually flows from His world to ours without beginning and without ending. Perhaps the utter reliance of science on the validity of the First and Third Laws of Thermodynamics[3] of classical physics needs to be re-evaluated. Our universe is really an unfamiliar universe operating with countless laws as yet unknown to us residing in a hidden but consistent set of symbols as yet undiscovered.

The energy of our universe is continually being recycled for reuse of some kind. God is the greatest of conservationists; nothing in His creation goes to waste or is completely annihilated. If each created thing were subject to absolute annihilation, the eventual outcome would be a universe in which all matter/energy simply disappeared. When we consider energy/mass transformations we know that basic matter, once created, is combined and recombined in an infinitude of forms. Form, structure and order are what define a universe both for science and for religion, not chaos and disorder.

Throughout existence unique atomic formations are endless. 'Abdu'l-Bahá tells us that nature never repeats herself in any one of her created forms. Science has also discovered that every stone, every flower, every animal and every human carries its own individual stamp of identity. A random or accidental creation could not result in these unique combinations for it would have no way of 'knowing' what not to repeat. We have been given a universe so intelligently designed and displaying such awesome originality, wisdom, and artistry that its abundant evidence, from the single atom to each human being, is obvious for all to see.

The Bahá'í conceptualization of how the matter of the universe is brought into existence is best explained by the journey of the ubiquitous and primordial atom. Unhindered, it alone freely crosses all creational boundaries to generate the probabilities that compete for existence in a dynamic, evolutionary and ordered arena of timelessness. 'Abdu'l-Bahá stated that every atom has equal opportunity to express all the virtues or attributes in each kingdom of existence. This initial condition of equilibrium, however, is not permanent, since 'mindful' energy eventually materializes into specific structure and order. Rather than assuming a universe based upon chance, the more accurate description might be that of *guided probability*, an idea we will now explore.

The Journey of the Atom

The illustration below may help us to visualize the 'journey of the atom' as it manifests all the Divine attributes and virtues emanating from the bounty of God. We will take this journey as spiritual theoreticians with a hypothetical hydrogen atom as our guide into the chain-linked world of being and explore each level with our inner eyes.

The illustration shows that each gradient is identified both by its own special 'sign from God', or attribute, as well as its fundamental purpose. To make it easier to follow, each 'sign' has been notated as a 'plus value', with each level carrying its own

51

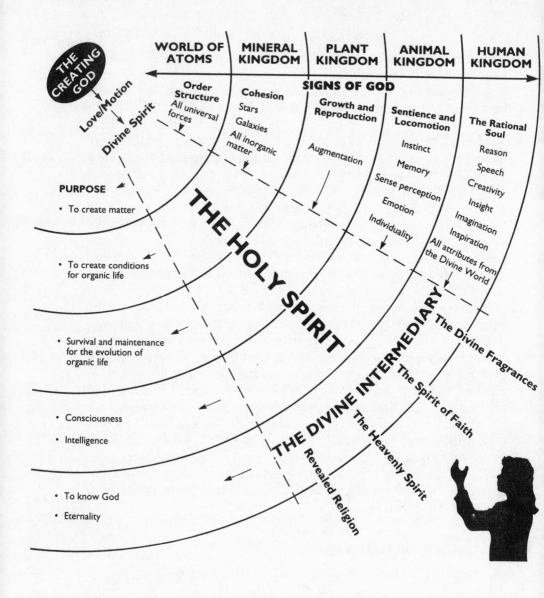

WORLD OF ATOMS	MINERAL KINGDOM	PLANT KINGDOM	ANIMAL KINGDOM	HUMAN KINGDOM

THE CREATING GOD

Love/Motion

Divine Spirit

SIGNS OF GOD

Order Structure
All universal forces

Cohesion
Stars
Galaxies
All inorganic matter

Growth and Reproduction

Augmentation

Sentience and Locomotion

Instinct

Memory

Sense perception

Emotion

Individuality

The Rational Soul

Reason

Speech

Creativity

Insight

Imagination

Inspiration

All attributes from the Divine World

THE HOLY SPIRIT

THE DIVINE INTERMEDIARY

The Divine Fragrances

The Spirit of Faith

The Heavenly Spirit

Revealed Religion

PURPOSE

• To create matter

• To create conditions for organic life

• Survival and maintenance for the evolution of organic life

• Consciousness
• Intelligence

• To know God
• Eternality

'Man is the sum of creation.'
'Abdu'l-Bahá (*Paris Talks*, p. 51)

virtue or value, plus the value(s) from below it. Each scale of existence has its own particular degree of perfection to which it aspires, with the means to achieve it already encoded within the laws governing the hierarchy.

The Nuclear Kingdom

The first creational level is invisible to us, emerging from the World of God. Its existence is pure energy and it flows from His world to give life and form to our universe. This is the level in which all the primordial cosmic forces are energized in the strange and miraculous beginnings of the nuclear/atomic world.

What was one unified force divides into two, separating positive from negative, inchoate energy particles forever in tension and motion, first repelling and then attracting differing versions of themselves, manifesting one characteristic, then another. They dance and merge or disappear, flowing ceaselessly and explosively between chaos and order, caught between the world of 'is' and the world of 'becoming'. Their frenzied motion generates the necessary high temperatures to eject protons, electrons and neutrons into the void. In a universe of accident and chance these unformed energy masses would travel aimlessly, attracting and repelling in equal exchanges, able to form only temporary alliances with each other, returning the original symmetry to the unformed universe.

But in our model of the universe these infinite energized probability-states are guided into states of coherence and stability. Particulate energy is prevented from remaining in its original condition of oneness by those colossal strong/weak, active/passive forces which instead act upon these energy/masses in such a way that they will attract each other unequally in an astonishing and precise mathematical progression. These three types of particles of matter/energy – protons, electrons and neutrons – gravitate to form families of atoms and the more massive molecules of gases. This strong tendency for particles to attract unevenly allows heterogeneous matter to stabilize and form a coherent universe. The result is the 'sign of God' that manifests itself in this first creational level: order and structure, the very pillars of a visible universe called into being by Divine Law.

This complex marvel of universal order and structure has a

purpose, the purpose of the hierarchy itself, that of creating and sustaining the proper mix that will eventuate in all organic and inorganic matter. This open-ended goal, so ingeniously realized in this level, becomes the evident 'sign of God' in the next level, the mineral kingdom, where inorganic matter perfects itself and manifests those powerful forces that make visible the celestial dominions which we take so much for granted.

The Mineral Kingdom

On this level of phenomena all atoms cohere in the molecular combinations which form the particular complex compounds that coalesce to form the heavy matter in the galaxies populated by solar systems with their life-giving planets of molten rock, mountains and seas, and all manner of metals and liquids. God might have been satisfied to stop His creational process at this stage: creating matter out of non-matter and making the invisible visible would be a victory worthy of any creator. But inorganic existence, no matter how awe-inspiring, seems only to have set the stage, its mineral construction a preamble to further miracles. Another level of existence is needed to realize fully this kingdom's purpose and meaning. This purpose, in turn, will become the next kingdom's genesis.

Hidden in Mother Earth's layers of carbonaceous matter is her watery womb containing the germ of organic life. The biological sciences still grapple with explanations for not only how but why this metamorphosis transforms inanimate matter into living matter capable of self-evolution, self-organization and self-consciousness. It is the preparation for this miracle of life that is the very purpose of the mineral kingdom. Every planet in the universe makes the attempt to prepare the matrix that will allow organic life to emerge and evolve from non-biological matter. Some succeed and some do not.

The Plant Kingdom

Now existence has stepped into the domain of cellular life – the plant kingdom. Here the 'signs and evidences of God' are so profuse with colour, beauty and variety that we are in awe of nature's art forms. These two kingdoms, mineral and plant, work together in such close symbiotic relationship, each benefiting the other, that we cannot imagine them apart. In this kingdom nature shows off her dazzling brilliance and powers, assuming our admiration and appreciation. Even her laws seem to be imaginative applications of God's laws, as she translates His Will into His Bounty.

What distinguishes the basic characteristics of life in this gradient is the ability of each simple form to grow, augment itself and reproduce in kind. These 'plus values' constitute the very essence or spirit of every organism in this kingdom and are its perfections. Unlike the mineral that persists for aeons, the occupant in this chain of the unity of being must struggle for its survival, its maintenance relying completely upon water, the energy of light and warmth, and whatever else the immediate environment provides. Because it is alive, nature's law requires that it must adapt or die. The energy on this level is translated into perfecting the cycles of growth and reproduction so that the survival of the subsequent phyla of life may be ensured. This is the purpose of the plant kingdom – perfecting those basic biological mechanisms that will allow each living organism of the kingdom to follow to survive as individuals.

Of course, not all plant species which are introduced will survive. At this level, nature seems to delight in experimentation; indeed, in her quest for perfection, no greater laboratory exists to equal this one and so some species are discarded as new ones flourish. This seemingly purposeless whim of nature results in the significant changes and adaptations necessary for the collective evolution of the genus, and seems to be one more example of what we have called 'guided probability'.

The Animal Kingdom

Conscious life can evolve only when and where the mineral and plant kingdoms maintain a mutual system of reciprocity. Conscious life makes many demands upon the natural environment, just as the environment, in turn, can deal harshly with animal life. The outcome of this confrontation seems to be that the strong, the adaptive and the most clever life-forms will survive to evolve successfully over time.

The animal kingdom comes endowed with all the perfected characteristics of the mineral and plant kingdoms and in addition each member is invested with the 'plus values' of sentience and locomotion. For the first time all the perceptual senses have been introduced to allow each individual creature to survive either autonomously or cooperatively. Not only can life forms now move by their own power and volition, but each member exhibits its own particular instincts and intelligence, grace and beauty, strength and prowess. The miracle of procreation, especially in mammals, bonds the mother and infant, creates dependency, and marks the beginning of those positive emotions we call nurturing, affection, caring and sharing. This family bonding is the beginning of the social structure and all cultural behaviour.

But the perfections which can be realized on this level are physical ones, not cultural ones. Again we remind ourselves that the signs of God in each tier do not constitute the purpose of God for that tier. The purpose for this order of life is to establish the foundation for individual conscious intelligence and self-awareness. We *know* that the higher animals possess consciousness and intelligence, but they themselves are unable to reflect upon this; that is, the animal knows, but it does not know that it knows. The animal lives out its life in accordance with God's Will, but 'Abdu'l-Bahá points out that it does so blindly and with no awareness. Its intelligence is inferior because it is incomplete.

We also know that the higher orders of mammalian life share with us the basic emotional instincts of fear, anger and desire and that they lovingly care for their young. Some animals, including insects, organize complex social enclaves. At the same time we observe them attacking and killing each other for food, for mates or for territorial rights. We are also unhappily aware that humankind commits these very same acts for the same basic reasons. In the case of animal behaviour, however, consciousness acts instinctively without assigning a scale of moral values to approved or unapproved acts. Biologists have observed that most infant animals go through a learning process so that they may internalize the 'right way' of doing things, but they do not invent abstract concepts such as 'good and evil' to describe or account for right or wrong actions.

'Right and wrong' can be defined as proper and improper behaviour culturally transmitted and learned, and our respect and observance of it (or lack of it) is carried out with the same dispatch as the higher animal. But abstract ideas that foster and shape moral behaviour must be products of a higher consciousness and a shared base of accumulated knowledge that must be diligently learned by each member of society over a period of many years. Learned moral and ethical behaviour may very well be the yardstick by which the animal and human family can be separated. We will speak more about these issues in a subsequent chapter.

The animal kingdom supplies ample evidence of the variety of individuation and specialization of its members; this means that often individual behaviour will be unpredictable. We can guess that these same patterns of behaviour will also characterize the members of the next level in even more complex ways. Our model also tells us that conscious intelligence will have been perfected so that it will manifest itself in remarkable ways. What possible 'plus value' is there left to express? And to what end is its purpose directed in this final kingdom of creation?

The Human Kingdom

'Abdu'l-Bahá introduces us to the occupants of this level in this passage:

> God has created all earthly things under a law of progression in material degrees, but He has created man and endowed him with powers of advancement toward spiritual and transcendental kingdoms. He has not created material phenomena after His own image and likeness, but He has created man after that image and with potential power to attain that likeness . . . He has brought forth everything necessary for the life of this world, but man is a creation intended for the reflection of divine virtues. Consider that the highest type of creation below man is the animal, which is superior to all degrees of life except man. Manifestly, the animal has been created for the life of this world. Its highest virtue is to express excellence in the material plane of existence . . . When it is characterized by the attributes of physical health, when its physical forces are in working order, when food and surrounding conditions minister to its needs, it has attained the ultimate perfection of its kingdom. But man does not depend upon these things for his virtues. No matter how perfect his health and physical powers, if that is all, he has not yet risen above the degree of a perfect animal. Beyond and above this, God has opened the doors of ideal virtues and attainments before the face of man.[4]

According to the Bahá'í teachings, *Homo sapiens* occupies a kingdom distinct from and superior to the animal. Just as we do not expect to see minerals evolving into plants, or plants into animals, we should be suspicious of any theory that allows a member of the animal kingdom to evolve into a new and distinct species that creates its own hierarchy of life. It might be argued that there are several enigmatic forms of inorganic and organic existence that appear to be crossing borders and at one time or another have puzzled science as to type. For example, crystalline growth, coral reefs, slime moulds, even the great apes, all of these forms possess certain characteristics that seem to fit either one or another level and might be seen as 'proof' of certain populations evolving from a lower tier to a higher. But the biological sciences have placed all these examples in their proper niches and we can see them for what they are – not crossovers but links between kingdoms. Each hints at the characteristics that describe the kingdom above it. A possible explanation might be that these links were necessary to nature's phylogenic blueprint for perfecting particular traits or preventing certain defects before they could be transmitted to successive levels. Whatever the reason, the Bahá'í explanation of biological evolution does not admit to members of one level evolving into the next with 'missing links'. These links are not missing at all; they are secure members of the lower order, not higher, and do not exist in some mysterious, hidden limbo between the two.

Dramatic variation has occurred from the very beginning to separate one life form from another in definable ways that are both biological and behavioural. It may very well be true that all organic life evolved from one primordial parental cell billions of years ago, as 'Abdu'l-Bahá also suggests (although not as an accidental and spontaneous occurrence), confirming that all life forms do, in fact, share a common, but extremely remote, ancestor. So it should not surprise us to learn that just as differentiation has created special gradients of life that are not only dissimilar but also superior to others, it has also created life forms with genetic structures so similar as to make humans first cousins to the African chimpanzee. But this information does not constitute a proof of a shared family descent; instead it seems to have confused the issue as much as it has shed light on it. Many evolutionary biologists, given the amount of contradictory data currently available to them, are still cautious about espousing the 'recent common ancestry theory' of humans and apes. What they do agree upon is the basic genetic unity of all organic life.

The scientific explanation for speciation, both general and specific, also remains an enigma. Not only why species have proliferated, but why phylogenic differentiation should have occurred at all, is even more puzzling. Why did not the first cell of life evolve into one consistent phylum of one order, one family and one genus, with speciation then occurring at that point? If we try to solve this problem by simply ascribing these miraculous events to 'accidental spontaneity' then we are left with over a billion years of continual but purposeless spontaneity to account for. We might allow for the emergence of one or two simple life forms with this explanation, but even if only *one* life form had evolved, no matter how primitive, it would still deserve a better causal resolution than the ones that the biological sciences currently espouse in order to side-step the question of purpose and meaning in evolutionary progression.

If, in the future, mankind should discover a planet which has evolved only to the kingdom of plant life, it would do well to consider the possibility, suggested by 'Abdu'l-Bahá, of a world-in-waiting preparing itself for the advent of conscious, reasoning life. Most scientists contend that intelligent life, whether animal or human, may be more rare than common in our universe; therefore, secure on our planet, we should not accept as a given that every planet in the universe contains the completed Kingdoms of God. For those which are evolving towards this completion we need to question the scientist's contention that they are all 'accidental effects' wrought by a random process admitting of neither cause nor purpose. We should demand a better and more comprehensive explanation for organic genesis from our evolutionary biologists.

The Evolution of Man

Bahá'u'lláh and 'Abdu'l-Bahá say simply that the human being has always occupied a distinct evolutionary tier although his form and shape have evolved and changed over millions of years. Our fictional Circadians in Chapter One metamorphosed their evolutionary development *ex utero*. *Homo sapiens* duplicates his evolutionary progression while still inside his mother's womb. The Bahá'í teachings say that ontogeny is a fact. So even though in his first stage man was aquatic, and in a later stage may have appeared ape-like, he was never such an extraordinary member of the animal kingdom that he was able to evolve into the only unique life form capable of escaping one level and artificially creating his own personal and superior kindgom.

> The first answer to this argument is the fact that the animal having preceded man is not a proof of the evolution, change and alteration of the species, nor that man was raised from the animal world to the human world ... when we examine the vegetable kingdom, we see that the fruits of the different trees do not arrive at maturity at one time; on the contrary, some come first and others afterward. This priority does not prove that the later fruit of one tree was produced from the earlier fruit of another tree.[5]

When evolutionary biologists accept that the origin of the human family is not only distinct but has resulted in the culminating species of our planet, it will become clear that our evolution is not a descent but an ascent. Because all created things carry within them varying degrees of some of the same attributes God possesses, we can infer that human existence on this planet will share certain similarities to those intelligent life forms existing elsewhere in our universe. This implies as well that all other planetary 'chains of being' would maintain a like mutual energy-exchange with each other in order to sustain a dynamic environment for the evolution of their unique organisms. This kind of consistency also requires that in all inhabited worlds each level of life will also be distinct and separate, each carrying its own 'signs of God' and each exhibiting its own unique 'plus values'.

Our 'Sign from God'

Looking again at the illustration on page 52 we notice that man has received attributes and perfections almost out of proportion to the lower kingdoms. We humans have been endowed with the highest gift the Divine Spirit of God can bestow – perfected intelligence. In man, spirit is revealed as mind. Mind reasons and is consciously aware of its rationality. This precious gift is the 'sign from God' which both defines and separates the human kingdom from all others. Religions and philosophies have given it a special name: the rational soul. It makes possible the actualization of our powers of comprehension, creativity, insight, ideation, imagination, logic, inspiration, love, and all the higher emotions we equate with this highest of all kingdoms.

> When man allows the spirit, through his soul, to enlighten his understanding, then does he contain all Creation; because man, being the culmination of all that went before and thus superior to all previous evolutions, contains all the lower world within himself. Illumined by the spirit, through the instrumentality of the soul, man's radiant intelligence makes him the crowning-point of Creation.[6]

The Purpose of the Human Kingdom

Proving the existence and perfections of the soul is not the purpose of the human tier, however. Something else remains that has not yet been included as the goal of any previous kingdom, and this 'something else' becomes the final aim of all creation. Once this purpose is explained we will understand why God did not end His creational plan with the animal kingdom. In the beginning, this goal existed as a hidden spiritual abstraction, but now it is something we must stumble upon for ourselves. As for the animal, plant and mineral, they will never be able to discover what purpose their kingdoms serve, but for them it is not necessary that they know. In the human kingdom, however, each member ultimately addresses himself to this question of what is the purpose of life. His answer will depend upon how well he has read the clues nature supplies and how much attention he has directed to the answers that the Manifestations of God have given.

God did not fashion the universe and bring all creation into being that we do nothing more than be obedient to Him; plants and animals do this much better than we. More than obedience, He desires our love, for He has certainly shown and given His without cessation. He also yearns for us to have knowledge of Him, for He surely knows us better than we know ourselves. What useful purpose would it serve a Creator to remain totally unknown and unknowable to His highest creation? To that end His Divine Spirit has ignited our human spirit in order to love

61

and to know Him, and solve the riddle of our own creation. But will we ever be able to solve this riddle?

The Holy Manifestations of God alone have given us the clues for its solution. Born in this world, but hinting at the next, They promise us the gift of everlasting life. They explain that because each individual essence originates from the Spirit of God, it too is eternal. The purpose or goal of the human kingdom is to prove the eternalness of the human spirit or soul.

In man, each atom has fulfilled its highest potential and realized its greatest purpose. There is no new level left for it to go to, nor is there anything greater that it can express. Thus it returns to its original state, to its point of origin, where it will be recycled to begin again its eternal wanderings throughout all the kingdoms of creation until 'the end which hath no end'.

The non-material spirit of man, however, once molecular dissolution has taken place, is freed to continue its journey in a different state and condition. Unlike the atom, whose journey takes place in the visible universe, the soul's journey continues in the non-visible worlds of God where a new progression and new spiritual journey begin. Like everything in the universe, the soul seeks its source and yearns for its reunion with that ineffable Oneness. This innate desire allows each of us to work our own way towards God in an eternal approach that will never be completed but will always be the journey of endless attraction.

Without this goal the human kingdom would have a purpose no different from the animal's. The mystery of our purpose is embedded in all the 'signs of God' that give unique definition to human life and experience. The clues are synecdochical analogies and imperfect metaphors that attempt to picture a concealed realm that we can discover both within us and outside us. Beyond symbolism is the certitude that knowledge of the highest and most perfect kingdom can be received only by the highest order of life, the species endowed with the perfections of a rational soul.

5

The Soul by Any Other Name

Man is in the highest degree of materiality, and at the beginning of spirituality – that is to say, he is the end of imperfection and the beginning of perfection. He is at the last degree of darkness, and at the beginning of light; that is why it has been said that the condition of man is the end of the night and the beginning of day, meaning that he is the sum of all the degrees of imperfection, and that he possesses the degrees of perfection ... Not in any other of the species in the world of existence is there such a difference, contrast, contradiction and opposition as in the species of man ... Briefly, all the perfections and virtues, and all the vices, are qualities of man.[1]

The rational soul – that is to say the human spirit – has neither entered this body nor existed through it ... On the contrary, the rational soul is the substance through which the body exists. The personality of the rational soul is from its beginning ... but the state and the personality of the rational soul may be strengthened in this world; it will make progress and will attain to the degrees of perfection, or it will remain in the lowest abyss of ignorance, veiled and deprived from beholding the signs of God.[2]

Further Problems of Definition

We now know that the human soul is the highest 'sign of God' in the ontological chain of existence and that it is a creation of the Divine Spirit/Energy, linking Essence with essence. We can sympathize with the difficulties religious philosophers have had in trying to prove the existence of the soul, to define it and to describe its state and condition. To a large extent, it has been the indiscriminate use of the word 'soul' that is responsible for our failure to grasp the meaning behind it. Another problem has been that there is no simple definition of the human soul. As we shall see, exploring the word turns out to be the same as exploring the subject. In fact we shall soon discover that the word itself is superfluous; its meaning can be explained in other, less ambiguous, terms.

Bahá'u'lláh was repeatedly asked for explanations and definitions of this invisible soul, just as 'Abdu'l-Bahá's European and American audiences were to ask Him the same questions years later. Their answers weave an intricate conceptualization which results in a definition of almost panoramic dimensions. Both Bahá'u'lláh's and 'Abdu'l-Bahá's explanations include many layers of significance because what we regard as our 'soul' applies to so many subjective levels.

For example, in one place Bahá'u'lláh writes: 'It is a divine energy, a substance, simple, and self-subsistent.'[3] In another passage He writes:

> Verily I say, the human soul is exalted above all egress and regress. It is still, and yet it soareth; it moveth, and yet it is still. It is, in itself, a testimony that beareth witness to the existence of a world that is contingent, as well as to the reality of a world that hath neither beginning nor end.[4]

'Abdu'l-Bahá expands upon His Father's words to tell us that:

> The soul, like the intellect, is an abstraction. Intelligence does not partake of the quality of space, but is related to man's brain. The intellect resides there, but not materially . . . In the same way, though the soul is a resident of the body, it is not to be found in the body.[5]

> The spirit is changeless, indestructible. The progress and development of the soul, the joy and sorrow of the soul, are independent of the physical body.

> If we are caused joy or pain by a friend, if a love prove true or false, it is the soul that is affected. If our dear ones are far from us – it is the soul that grieves, and the grief or trouble of the soul may react on the body.

> Thus, when the spirit is fed with holy virtues, then is the body joyous; if the soul falls into sin, the body is in torment . . .

These are all things pertaining to the soul, and are not *bodily* ills. Thus, it is apparent that the soul, even as the body, has its own individuality. But if the body undergoes a change, the spirit need not be touched.[6]

When Bahá'u'lláh and 'Abdu'l-Bahá refer to the soul as a substance as well as an energy, they do not mean that it has a tangible or corporeal existence. In English, the word 'substance' has undergone changes in usage, although its dictionary definition remains true to the way the Greek and later European philosophers used the original word. Its closest approximation in meaning is our word 'essence'. It is also close in meaning to the Greek word *physis*, loosely translated as 'beingness', or 'what it means to be a thing'. Aristotle used 'substance' to connote the essential nature of created forms. Essence, or substance, then, refers to the invisible identity of a form, its unseen nature, which persists through time, change and transformations. The question that confronted the ancient philosophers was, did this 'substance' or 'beingness' also survive unchanged after death?

The Soul as Metaphor

If we cannot know the 'essence' of anything, how do we go about describing the nature of the human soul and substantiating its existence in a reasonable way? This presents the same kind of bafflement as that of asking someone who had never seen his reflection to describe his face. The solution may be the same – perhaps we need to look for a mirror that will reflect the true image of the human reality. This type of secondhand representation has been most often accomplished with some success by the use of analogies, symbolism and metaphors. For example, the following description combines all three linguistic devices and has been used with variations by both Eastern and Western writers to represent the condition of the soul in this life.

Imagine the body as analogous to an old-fashioned but finely-made carriage. The driver (the intellect) holds the reins (the will) to check the raw energy and passions of our spirited horses (the emotions). Only by working together as a unit can they arrive at their destination. Inside the carriage is a passenger – the reason and purpose the journey is being made at all – hidden and hardly visible even to the driver. Only the passenger knows the importance of the journey. It is, of course, the soul. At its destination, the passenger disembarks, for the first time able to leave the shelter and protection of the carriage, driver and horses, and continues on alone.

This metaphoric description gives us only an image for our elusive subject-matter, but it does not qualify as a definition. The strength of symbols and metaphors lies in their ability to present a picture of an abstraction that otherwise resists linguistic precision. Their weakness is that they show us reality as though looking 'through a glass darkly'. If we want to reconceptualize the soul it appears we will have to change both our language and our perspective concerning it. Once we do this, we should be well on our way to finding the mirror that will truly image the human spirit.

The Layered Definitions of Soul

The Bahá'í Writings reveal that the true nature of the soul encompasses every process of life and is, indeed, the basic motive force of life. It is not a 'something' residing passively somewhere inside the body waiting to be released in a pure and holy state at the hour of death. If we put together all that we have learned about the human soul in Chapter Four we can offer a reasonable definition that will be far different from anything we have previously imagined.

According to Bahá'u'lláh and 'Abdu'l-Bahá, the soul is a collectivity consisting of all those qualities and attributes endowed by the Divine Spirit that make us members of the human kingdom and no other. In particular, it encompasses all those special attributes and bestowals which in Chapter Four we called the 'plus values' that characterize and ignite the human condition. Scholars have always analyzed these qualities as separate properties arising from different aspects of human nature but without really accounting for them. Put simply, these characteristics describe what a human being is.

Ever since Descartes separated mind (soul) from body (matter) in the seventeenth century we have become psychologically disconnected in the West. Ironically, it was not Descartes's purpose to provide an irreconcilable separation of the spiritual from the corporeal; his intent was to reconcile the new Copernican view of heaven and earth with the medieval theology of the Catholic Church by providing reasonable arguments that would satisfy both positions. We have only recently, in the last few decades, begun to reconsider the possibility that spiritual, intellectual, emotional and even physical aspects of the human condition are all interrelated and interdependent and work together as one whole. Bahá'u'lláh explains how this collective reality operates as our rational faculty in the following passage:

> Consider the rational faculty with which God hath endowed the essence of man. Examine thine own self, and behold how thy motion and stillness, thy will and purpose, thy sight and hearing, thy sense of smell and power of speech, and whatever else is related to, or transcendeth, thy physical senses or spiritual perceptions, all proceed from, and owe their existence to, this same faculty. So closely are they related unto it, that if in less than the twinkling of an eye its relationship to the human body be severed, each and every one of these senses will cease immediately to exercise its function, and will be deprived of the power to manifest the evidences of its activity ... Through its manifestation all these names and attributes have been revealed, and by the suspension of its action they are all destroyed and perish.[7]

In another Tablet He wrote: 'Say, that spirit, mind, soul, hearing and sight are one, but differ through differing causes.'[8]

If the Divine Spirit can manifest itself in an almost infinite variety of created forms throughout the universe, then the human spirit, also carrying the miraculous powers of the Divine Spirit but on a much less grand scale, should also be able to manifest itself in a variety of unique combinations. If this is true, then we have discovered the secret of how individuals can differ from one another and be distinct and unique personalities. The one thing that connects us all and makes us alike is the expression of the Divine Spirit as the rational soul or mind. Mind as the awareness of self and others becomes the highest power of our human spirit. 'Abdu'l-Bahá explains this idea in his Tablet to Dr Forel:

> Now regarding the question whether the faculties of the mind and the human soul are one and the same. These faculties are but the inherent properties of the soul, such as the power of

imagination, of thought, of understanding; powers that are the essential requisites of the reality of man . . .[9]

His elaboration further defines the soul:

This much can be stated, that the reality of man is a pure and unknown essence constituting a depository emanating from the light of the Ancient Entity, God. This essence or soul of man because of its innate purity and its connection with the unseen Ancient Entity is old as regards time but new as regards individuality . . . It is the same reality which is given different names, according to the different conditions wherein it is manifested. Because of its relation to matter and the phenomenal world when it governs the physical functions of the body, it is called the human soul; when it manifests itself as the thinker, the comprehender, it is called the mind. And when it soars into the atmosphere of God and travels in the spiritual world it becomes designated as spirit.[10]

The Bahá'í explanation of the human soul changes our view of all living things. As spirit it elevates all existence, especially human existence, to the apex of a divine ontology. With this explanation even members of the lower orders of creation can be said to possess a 'soul' if by this we mean the particular identifying 'sign from God' that the Divine Spirit has imprinted within each created thing.

The above passage also informs us that the human soul/spirit comes into existence at the moment of conception, for this is when the Divine Spirit gives life through the joining of opposites, the active/passive or male/female aspects of its energy. 'Abdu'l-Bahá explains how this comes about.

. . . just as in the first birth the foetus comes forth from the matrix of the mother into the conditions of the human kingdom, even so the spirit of man must be born out of the matrix of naturalism, out of the baser nature, in order that he may comprehend the great things of the Kingdom of God. He must be born out of mother earth to find the everlasting life. . . . this collective reality, or spirit, of man, being born out of the world of nature, possessing the attributes of God, will continue to live forever in the eternal realm.[11]

Know thou that every soul is fashioned after the nature of God, each being pure and holy at his birth. Afterwards, however, the individuals will vary according to what they acquire of virtues or vices in this world.[12]

In the human [kingdom], worldly soul signifies the 'rational being, or mind'. This has a potential existence before its appearance in human life . . . through the mixture of elements and a wonderful combination, according to the natural order, law, conception, and birth, it appears with its identity.

   Be it known that to know the reality or essence of the soul of man is impossible, for, in order to know a thing, one must comprehend it, and since a thing cannot comprehend itself, to know one's self in substance or essence is impossible.[13]

Before conception there is only the Divine Spirit of God in which individual human identity exists as a potentiality. Conception is the moment when the Divine Energy enters the realm of separate self-recognition. Each new soul is born in a condition of purity. Infants are naturally purely good. It is only afterwards, 'Abdu'l-Bahá points out, that our problems begin.

The Transilient Nature of Man

If the spiritual essence of man is purely good, the question arises as to how people can also possess a baser nature. We have ample evidence that man can be bestial and cruel; he can also be quite ordinary and commonplace; in addition he can so elevate his nature as to be wise, compassionate and virtuous. Trying to understand and integrate these three shifting aspects of our human nature cause most of our self-identity problems. Our solution is to walk a psychological tightrope as we try to balance by not leaning too far either to the right or to the left. The majority of us travel precariously on this great middle road. Outwardly, we approve of Dr Jekyll, but inwardly we are obsessed with Mr Hyde, although most of us do not take the risks involved with experiencing either extreme. Unless labels are worn, we do not know who anyone is.

   So many inconsistencies in human behaviour confront us that even our questions perplex us. If it is true that each of us has a soul, then why doesn't it tell us who we are and what we should do? Or, if the soul is supposed to be innately pure, then why isn't everyone virtuous and good? And if it remains pure throughout eternity, then why should it matter what we do here and now?

Haven't we been told we are all equally saints and sinners, and that since God created us this way, He must intend that we remain this way?

The Two-Sided Mirror

When 'Abdu'l-Bahá was in Paris in 1912 He spoke eloquently on the nature of the human spirit and made it clear that the choices we make in life must be distinctive. Even though some deletions have been made in this rather short talk, most of what 'Abdu'l-Bahá said is included here.

> ... if the spiritual qualities of the soul, open to the breath of the Divine Spirit, are never used, they become atrophied, enfeebled, and at last incapable; whilst the soul's material qualities alone being exercised, they become terribly powerful – and the unhappy, misguided man becomes more savage, more unjust, more vile, more cruel, more malevolent than the lower animals themselves. All his aspirations and desires being strengthened by the lower side of the soul's nature, he becomes more and more brutal, until his whole being is in no way superior to that of the beasts that perish. Men such as this plan to work evil, to hurt and to destroy; they are entirely without the spirit of Divine compassion, for the celestial quality of the soul has been dominated by that of the material.[14]

But this Hobbesian view of man is like seeing ourselves from the backside of a mirror. Its image distorts us. Seen from the front, our image is as different as night is from day.

> If, on the contrary, the spiritual nature of the soul has been so strengthened that it holds the material side in subjection, then does man approach the Divine; his humanity becomes so glorified that the virtues of the Celestial Assembly are manifested in him; he radiates the Mercy of God, he stimulates the spiritual progress of mankind, for he becomes a lamp to show light on their path.[15]

'Abdu'l-Bahá ends his talk by integrating man's two reflections in a full-dimensional portrayal of man's fundamental humanness:

> Some men's lives are solely occupied with the things of this world; their minds are so circumscribed by exterior manners

and traditional interests that they are blind to any other realm of existence, to the spiritual significance of all things! They think and dream of earthly fame, of material progress. Sensuous delights and comfortable surroundings bound their horizon, their highest ambitions centre in successes of worldly conditions and circumstances! They curb not their lower propensities; they eat, drink, and sleep! Like the animal, they have no thought beyond their own physical well-being. It is true that these necessities must be despatched. Life is a load which must be carried on while we are on earth, but the cares of the lower things of life should not be allowed to monopolize all the thoughts and aspirations of a human being. The heart's ambitions should ascend to a more glorious goal, mental activity should rise to higher levels! Men should hold in their souls the vision of celestial perfection, and there prepare a dwelling-place for the inexhaustible bounty of the Divine Spirit.[16]

How easy it would be for us to realize this goal if the human spirit came equipped with innate knowledge, particularly that of good and evil. But its only innate knowledge is its desire to return to its point of origin and re-enter the world of Spirit and to recognize what will aid it in this goal. Nor is the soul our wise conscience, whispering instructions to us direct from God. If it possessed such a power there would be no need for the Divine Manifestations and their revelations, nor would there have been any reason for the human spirit to take on a corporeal form at all, for it would have entered this world already in a condition of immediate and effortless perfection. The human species shares with all life forms the instinctual self-survival trait realized in the struggle to develop its highest potentialities.

Imprints of the Soul

Bahá'u'lláh and 'Abdu'l-Bahá also remind us that the soul/spirit of every human being is created equal and identical. The Divine Spirit breathes into each living individual the same portion of that individual's identifying spirit. Thus, no human being receives any more or any less of the Divine Spirit than anyone else, whether male or female, white or black, primitive or advanced. Even if we use as examples humankind as it existed a million years ago, or humankind as it will exist a million years

71

hence, we are still talking about the same human spirit. Every soul is given, and will continue to be given, the same potentialities and susceptibilities that define the full human spectrum of seeking, thinking, feeling and doing. As each being evolves and matures these spiritual powers unfold.

What makes us all different are the almost infinite ways these potentialities manifest themselves as our individual capabilities, talents and skills. All these capacities, as we learn early in life, although identical in kind are not identical in degree. Is there any explanation for this unequal distribution? In the long run, shouldn't all our differences combine to create a balanced but dynamic gene pool? And do the inequalities that arise from differing capacities impede our spiritual growth? If we can shed further light on the nature of the human soul, perhaps some of these questions will begin to answer themselves.

Our human life processes rely upon a tremendous store of reserve energy. All our potentialities lie latent within this reservoir where they will be developed completely, moderately or perhaps not at all. How they reveal themselves forms the basis of individual human behaviour.

When spirit is born into the world of matter it manifests almost immediately a unique individuality. This 'true self' is determined as much by genetic combinations as by the mysterious properties of Spirit which have come together at a particular time and place in history to create a particular and distinct human life. Our parents, ethnic group, nation, education, etc., are just as powerful factors in shaping this once-only self that is *ourself*. 'Abdu'l-Bahá observed that in a family of many children, all raised in the same environment and with the same upbringing and education, each will exhibit his own character and develop his own personality; each will respond differently to the same conditions of life. There are as many causes to account for such individual differences as there are explanations and they are as complicated and contradictory as human behaviour itself.

The Inner Spiritual Core

Although our inner core of identity is very strong at birth, it is also very pliable and vulnerable to outside influences, since it is these outside influences that will shape its development. It is therefore easy for child-raising techniques to change this pristine condition into fixed family and cultural behaviour patterns that allow children to become acceptable socialized adults. It is a process designed to toughen us so that we can survive and function in our particular social environment. We call these acquired inner protective devices our 'personality', or the image we present to the public.

Personality consists of the glossy overlays with which we cover and protect our inner and private self and which become ever more opaque and unchanging with age. The more our acquired personality enlarges and flourishes, the more our innate character starves and languishes. Our true self eventually becomes so smothered from all the protection we give it that we no longer remember or know who or what it really is. We only know that something important is missing, even lost, in our lives and we do not know how to get it back. As a result, our true inner nature, the character we were born with, ceases to grow.

> Man is said to be the greatest representative of God, and he is the Book of Creation because all the mysteries of beings exist in him. If he comes under the shadow of the True Educator and is rightly trained, he becomes the essence of essences, the light of lights, the spirit of spirits; he becomes the centre of the divine appearances, the source of spiritual qualities, the rising-place of heavenly lights, and the receptacle of divine inspirations. If he is deprived of this education he becomes the manifestation of satanic qualities, the sum of animal vices, and the source of all dark conditions.[17]

All the expressions of the soul are powerful. Its powers are both active and passive; it can magnify life's experiences or merely absorb them. It can also become so abased from wrong signals identifying reality that it can become a 'darkened light', as 'Abdu'l-Bahá termed it. Much like the stomach that attempts to digest whatever food it is given, the soul will also attempt to digest whatever 'food' we give it.

Now we have made an unexpected discovery: the mirror we have been seeking has been right here all along! The soul is not the image *in* the mirror; it *is* the mirror! Even though the human spirit is pure essence, at birth it is so unblemished and chaste that it acts as a mirror reflecting clearly its true

73

attributes. It is no ordinary mirror. It retains every image it will ever receive. As a result, as we grow to become adults, distorted reflections of reality streak and blemish its surface. Through our individual thoughts and actions it becomes what we make of it.

The Path to Liberation

What religions call spiritual salvation or liberation is the freeing of the soul from its captivity to its lower nature. How to do this has been laid out by the Holy Teachers as a distinct path. They are the perfect mirrors in which we can see the perfect image of being. If we want perfectibility to be more than just a possibility, we will have to travel this path. Even though this journey has never been denied to anyone who has genuinely sought it, it requires many preparations. It is the most difficult journey we will ever make. Successes and failures in life are measured differently here. One of its prerequisites is like no other – the unification of self. Before that can be achieved, of course, we first must acquire knowledge of what the self is – especially our own particular self. How much can we learn about the fundamental nature of self by studying fundamental human behaviour? The Bahá'í teachings indicate that this is a good place to start.

6

The Paradoxical Nature of the
Unity of Opposites

You have asked why it was necessary for the soul that was from God to make this journey back to God? Would you like to understand the reality of this question just as I teach it, or do you wish to hear it as the world teaches it? . . .

The reality underlying this question is that the evil spirit, Satan or whatever is interpreted as evil, refers to the lower nature in man. The baser nature is symbolized in various ways. In man there are two expressions: one is the expression of nature; the other, the expression of the spiritual realm. The world of nature is defective . . . God has never created an evil spirit; all such ideas and nomenclature are symbols expressing the mere human or earthly nature of man . . .

Man must walk in many paths and be subjected to various processes in his evolution upward. Physically he is not born in full stature but passes through consecutive stages of foetus, infant, childhood, youth, maturity and old age. Suppose he had the power to remain young throughout his life. He then would not understand the meaning of old age and could not believe it existed. If he could not realize the condition of old age, he would not know that he was young . . . If there were no wrong, how would you recognize the right? If it were not for sin, how would you appreciate virtue? If evil deeds were unknown, how could you commend good actions? If sickness did not exist, how would you understand health? Evil is nonexistent; it is the absence of good. Sickness is the loss of health; poverty, the lack of riches . . . Without knowledge there is ignorance; therefore, ignorance is simply the lack of knowledge. Death is the absence of life. Therefore, on the one hand, we have existence; on the other, nonexistence, negation or absence of existence.

Briefly, the journey of the soul is necessary. The pathway of life is the road which leads to divine knowledge and attainment. Without training and guidance the soul could never progress beyond the conditions of its lower nature, which is ignorant and defective.[1]

Paradoxes

When we are presented with a logical statement or idea that seems contradictory either to the accepted wisdom or to our own internal schematic, we usually dismiss it as being absurd. This, of course, is one way to define a paradox. But what keeps a true paradox from being rejected as an absurdity is that the paradox continues to nag at us and we come back to it, puzzling over it; for beneath the apparent contradictory reasoning, a different way of looking at the idea emerges that is just as valid. Again, it is our limited perception of reality that is the culprit. Paradoxes seem to exist in other layers of reality that are not readily seen. Most of the paradoxes we are familiar with are those ferretted out by mathematicians as puzzles and games to be solved intellectually. We do not often view ourselves, our friends or our cultures as being even more complicated paradoxes than games of mathematical logic.

Recent refinements in the methodologies of the behavioural and psychological sciences have given us accurate patterns of personality traits that can be inventoried and correlated by psychological testing. It seems that now these practitioners can also sit down with a piece of paper and figure out much of our human paradoxical behaviour by manipulating words and numbers.

We are, all of us, studies in the contradiction of opposites and in the unity of opposites. This frustrating truth is a condition of the world of relativities. Human behaviour expresses itself in what sometimes seems to be a combat zone where conflicting inclinations battle for control over our natures. As 'the sum of all creation' we carry characteristics that we describe as 'animal' and 'angelic' and an in-between state that attempts to integrate these two extremes. As a result, we seem to spend our lives warring with ourselves and others, agonizing over our weaknesses and faults, our failures and successes, and what might be good and what might be evil. So far, the complexities, the contradictions, and the genius of life and human behaviour have been only partially explained and resolved. We will explore the Bahá'í teachings further to see if they can offer us additional clues as to why human beings behave as they do.

The Polarities of Human Expression

Our exploration begins with the observation that human actions seem to move between the polarities of active-passive and positive-negative behaviour. We do or we don't; we speak and act rashly, or we are cautious and circumspect; we like some things but do not like others, etc. In between these plus and minus behavioural responses are a variety of grey or intermediary areas open to us. If we examine this idea further, we notice that many of our responses seem to be expressed along a positive/negative continuum ranging from more to less, do's to don'ts, constructive to destructive, ardent to indifferent, etc. These behavioural responses, particularly emotional ones, exhibit themselves in varying degrees of intensity of psychological energy that could be measured, had we the instruments to do so. Even though emotional range testing is not common, we are all familiar with IQ tests for determining types or degrees of intelligence measured on a graduated scale.

Except for instinctual reactions, there seems to be no 'one response or no response' human behaviour that occurs naturally. Rather there is an almost boundless spectrum of intellectual and emotional responses that can be expressed in a vast range between these negative and positive modes. For example, there are varying degrees of love that we can feel, as well as its opposite expression of hate; we can tell little lies or big lies, and we can be more or less sympathetic. There are varying degrees of industriousness and of laziness, of joy and of grief, of tranquillity and of anxiety. All such pairs of opposites exist side by side in every one of us. Why these intellectual and emotional conditions should exist as polarities causing us to choose between and among them has seldom been considered. We shall soon discover that there are very good reasons for possessing such a large range of positive/negative responses and that they largely explain the contradictions in human behaviour.

77

The Origin of the Religious Concept of Good and Evil

Even though we can dismiss the simplification of naming actions (or objects) as being either 'good' or 'bad', we cannot dismiss the West's preoccupation with its simplistic concept of good and evil. Civilizations, past and present, have tussled with their philosophical and moral implications to the point where, currently, there does not seem to be anything new that can be added. It is also true that contemporary philosophy has disguised the problem of good and evil, which it sees primarily as a religious question, to talk instead about ethics, not in any classical sense, but relegated to the changing rules of conduct that are the product of social mores and cultural relativism. Since this type of treatment is superficial at best and euphemistic at worst, the discipline of philosophy finds itself confronted with students of philosophy who continue to be obsessed with questions, not about good, but about evil.

Evil, as an omnipotent, omnipresent force, found its way into Western Judeo-Christian civilization by way of Zoroastrianism, a major religion at least three thousand years old. Zarathustra described the forces at work within the universe and within man as being one and the same, possessing both a positive and a negative side. He personified these forces as agents of light and darkness responsible for good and evil, so that they would be more easily understood by His followers who were unlettered, untutored, and mostly simple, peace-loving agriculturists. Being worshippers of nature, they were also superstitious and spiritually unsophisticated. Zarathustra's elevated concept of the universal unity of opposites would have been difficult to comprehend without the aid of simple stories describing metaphorically the relationships between humankind and God.

Ahura Mazda, Zarathustra's name for God, was never two gods; He was always one. Ahriman personified the opposing force in the universe, as necessary as destruction is to construction, as darkness is to light, as death is to life. This 'opposing force' could be used to explain animistic spirits as well as man's cruel behaviour – in short, all those things people feared and called evil. Zarathustra's followers could live in accordance with this explanation, trying to do and to be better, because Zarathustra taught that the force of darkness or evil could be battled and overcome, just as God always overcame it at the end

78

of His cycles. This personified force became the West's Satan, the devil, and all the other names we have borrowed or invented that have come to us through Judaism, Christianity, Islam and a host of other lesser Near Eastern religions. In the Bahá'í religion, the word 'Satan' is occasionally used to refer to anything that people call evil.

We can see how easily a sophisticated explanation of man's baser nature as being a natural expression of negative forces at work everywhere in the universe could become subverted and misunderstood and at last over-simplified by those who were raised, not by thought, but by superstition and magic. Such ideas of good and evil still abound throughout our world in people still shackled by these same primitive misconceptions.

The Non-Existence of Evil

It is not a new idea that the Bahá'í teachings offer on the non-existence of evil; it is the explanation of the idea that is new. 'Abdu'l-Bahá considers this question in two parts: things that exist as material objects and those that have an intellectual reality. He says:

Intellectual things are those which have no outward existence but are conceptions of the mind. For example, mind itself is an intellectual thing which has no outward existence. All man's characteristics and qualities form an intellectual existence and are not sensible.

Briefly, the intellectual realities, such as all the qualities and admirable perfections of man, are purely good, and exist. Evil is simply their non-existence ... In the same way, the sensible realities are absolutely good, and evil is due to their non-existence – that is to say, blindness is the want of sight, deafness is the want of hearing, poverty is the want of wealth, illness is the want of health, death is the want of life, and weakness is the want of strength.[2]

He is not saying that absence-of conditions do not exist but only that they exist by default. We do not say, for example, wealth is the want of poverty, sight is the want of blindness, etc. The true reality is the positive condition and its opposite can only be defined in terms of the 'real' condition. Put another way, the negative is defined in terms of what the positive is not. Light is not defined by darkness, but darkness is defined as the

79

absence of light. One is the negation of the other; its non-existence is for definitional purposes only. We would not tell a person living in poverty that his poverty was non-existent; what is non-existent is his wealth. Because in this case wealth does not exist, the void or lack is filled by a word, 'poverty'. As a condition, it is very real.

An analogy is that of a tree that casts a shadow. The reality is the tree; the shadow can exist only so long as the tree exists – it exists by default. A Bahá'í educator some years ago put this idea into a psychological framework, saying that 'every vice is the shadow of its virtue'.[3] The Latin root word for our word 'vice', in fact, means lack of, or deficiency.

As for material objects, 'Abdu'l-Bahá states that all created objects are intrinsically good. But material objects, having been created in the world of relativities, may be viewed as good by some and evil by others, depending upon who is doing the viewing. To itself, for example, the scorpion is purely good.

Abstractions like good and evil exist as mental constructs; however, in this case, the construct has been more useful than successful. It has been more successful in courts of law than in religious theology where it has become not only ambiguous but muddled. The theological question was, if God is purely good and His creation purely good, how is it He allowed evil to exist? To be fair, this philosophical conundrum first occurred to the Greeks. One thing we can be sure of, if any philosophical question persists over time, it does so either because of how we have applied the rules of the grammar of logic to answer it, or because we have not properly asked it in the first place.

To define the word 'good' at all we must define it in relative, comparative terms for it has no 'absolute' definition and so cannot truly be ascribed as a name or quality of God. It is a human adjective describing relative states and conditions set up by the requirements of the culture. Religious philosophies often use this overworked adjective because it has become so embedded in our language systems that it can set the stage, so to speak, for deeper discourse. But so long as we ask the wrong questions about God, the universe and ourselves, we continue to set ourselves up for perplexities and wrong answers. It is not the problem of good and evil that is pivotal, but how the interplay of constantly shifting positive and negative qualities shapes our behaviour.

Evil as Imperfection

Bahá'u'lláh and 'Abdu'l-Bahá state repeatedly that absolute perfection lies with God only. His universe has been perfectly fashioned and it sustains itself in perfect fashion. Everything in creation 'works' for its own benefit as well as for the benefit of everything else. The interrelatedness and interconnectedness of all existence display this mutual reciprocity in ways science is only beginning to understand. Also, each level of reality functions perfectly; however, the individual components that inhabit each level do not. Nonetheless, every created thing has been given the means for reaching its own innate degree of perfection. This possibility is itself a perfect way for the Creator to define His relationship to His creation. Because perfection in the relative world exists as a potentiality, its attainment is possible only over a long passage of time with great effort and with the right conditions. This idea also tells us that perfection is the positive quality or state and that imperfection is its lack. 'Abdu'l-Bahá defined evil as imperfection. In between perfection and imperfection (good and evil), of course, are many degrees.

Bahá'u'lláh wrote that nothing that we call evil ever came directly from God, but that 'every evil thing is from yourselves'.[4] 'Evil' actions arise from the misuse of positive or 'good' behaviour to re-emerge in the negative range as wilful, destructive behaviour. The practitioner of evil has written a new script for himself in order to justify the bizarre reality his distorted imagination has invented. The lack of good actions is filled, not by a negative evil force, but by the negative behavioural responses that he has chosen.

A passage describing the dysfunctional nature of evil written by the Bahá'í scholar J.E. Esslemont is quoted here to help clarify the Bahá'í position.

> According to the Bahá'í philosophy it follows from the doctrine of the unity of God that there can be no such thing as positive evil. There can only be One Infinite. If there were any other power in the universe outside of or opposed to the One, then the One would not be Infinite. In the realm of created things, however, there is variety – variety of light and shade, of colour, of consistence, of taste, of smell. Among human beings there is variety of physical strength, of health, of intelligence, of courage, of every possible faculty and attribute. With regard to

every one of these qualities however the differences among different people are differences of degree, not of essence . . . A bad man is a man with the higher side of his nature still underdeveloped. If we are selfish, the evil is not in our love of self – all love, even self love, is good, is divine. The evil is that we have such a poor, inadequate, misguided love of self and such a lack of love for others and for God. We look upon ourself as only a superior sort of animal and foolishly pamper our lower nature as we might pamper a pet dog – with worse results in our own case than in that of the dog. We may be brilliantly intellectual with regard to material things but we are blind to the things of the spirit and lacking in the higher and nobler part of life. Evil is always the lack of life. If the lower side of man's nature is disproportionately developed, the remedy is not less life for that side, but *more* life for the higher side, so that the balance may be restored. 'I am come,' said Christ, 'that ye may have life and that ye may have it more abundantly.' That is what we all need – life, more life, the life that is life indeed![5]

Is Evil Innate?

Sometimes it seems to us that some individuals are 'born evil', for whatever reasons we may ascribe. 'Abdu'l-Bahá explains how this cannot be. At birth the infant's primary concern is to survive. The human baby cries and shows distress, signalling one of two basic instincts: fear or desire. His distress tells his mother that all is not right; he is either fearful, angry or desirous of something. To desire is to ask for something more and is a praiseworthy quality when it is used suitably, since from the moment of birth we have both needs and wants. As adults we may desire education, a satisfying career, a husband or wife, friends and a certain amount of material wealth. Desires such as these are praiseworthy and need not prevent us from attaining our spiritual birthright.

Fear is also necessary to our healthy survival; it is a biological communication that signals danger to the system. As basic instincts, fear and desire are both positive and good; it is only when their objectives are misdirected to what is unlawful, excessive or harmful to self or others that they become destructive.

Anger is felt when a need or want is not met. It arises from our thwarted desires. The Buddha, of course, had much to say on this subject.

We can speculate that fear and desire are our two most basic emotional instincts which, as infants, motivated us on our very deepest levels and which are responsible for shaping most of our adult behaviour through our unconscious secondary responses to them. As examples we can cite the infant's unconscious fear of abandonment or of rejection by his mother which later transfers to his relationships with people. A fear that mother's love may be removed may later unconsciously prevent him from forming adult loving relationships, the distrust of his mother's behaviour mutating into a general distrust of people. An infant who is deprived of basic emotional needs and wants may later release his anger against society in criminal acts. In others, this suppressed anger may emerge less negatively as a desire to please everyone in order to elicit attention and love from others. These two basic instincts weave intricate emotional behaviour patterns in all of us, patterns we are just beginning to understand.

These examples of adult responses growing out of the infant's perception of reality need not lead to neurotic behaviour. Depending upon our other inner and outer resources and strengths, these infantile reactions can be subverted and redirected into effective and responsible responses to life. The Bahá'í teachings help us to realize this shift in a practical way.

'Abdu'l-Bahá states that the worst of all acquired responses is the habit of lying because it is the foundation of all vices and all human evils. Nonetheless, He goes on to say, if a doctor should tell a sick patient that he is getting better, even though he knows these words are contrary to the truth, yet 'they may become the consolation of the patient and the turning-point of the illness. This is not blameworthy.'[6] Does this mean 'Abdu'l-Bahá approved a double standard for honesty? As we shall soon see, human traits and qualities are not exhibited as either/or responses. 'Abdu'l-Bahá's message goes far beyond our ordinary interpretations of what determines standards of moral behaviour.

He asks us to accept and understand our human complexities on a level worthy of our grasp. Precedents, or traditional social norms, may or may not create the 'proper' response; similar situations may be resolved more constructively by an awareness of varying levels of ethical responses. Still, the question that should be addressed here is not reducible to 'situational ethics'. We need to determine how we can acquire the right kind of knowledge so that we may know which particular response will expand our innate qualities to their fullest and most ideal expressions and provide the most benefits. Answering this inquiry philosophically is, as usual, easier than accomplishing it in action.

The Positive/Negative Continuum

We go back to the idea that every quality has a full range of expression from positive to negative. Although we name the negative expression with one word and its positive expression with another, it is but one quality that is being expressed. Our understanding of human behaviour could make rapid progress if all the differing words in our language were changed to accommodate this truth. It would help psychologists find new insights into both neurotic and normal behaviours. This notion lends itself to a thermometer-scale called a *semantic differential* that illustrates how 'pairs of opposites' exist as a unity, and how

QUALITY

BLAMEWORTHY ◄——— WORTHY ———► PRAISEWORTHY

+1 +2 +3 +4 +5 +6 +7 +8 +9 +10
_____
−10 −9 −8 −7 −6 −5 −4 −3 −2 −1

HATE ◄——————— LIKING ———————► LOVE

our expression of any genuine quality slides back and forth in varying degrees of intensity as we respond to the experiences of life.

Our first example in the diagram is a word used by 'Abdu'l-Bahá in many of his explanations of human qualities, the only word in the English language that is the same for all three states of the condition we call 'worthiness'. The diagram omits the zero range, or total absence of any quality, since, even at birth, our mental and emotional pages are not blank. This beginning state lying between positive and negative is a kind of 'hovering' state and is our basic psychological acknowledgement of any particular quality. An analogy which might make descriptive sense would be an automobile in idle gear. Our emotions and thoughts are never turned off completely, and even in quiet relaxation we are in a natural benign state hovering between thought and action. This state can be charted as a +1. In this state we are all innately 'worthy' beings. (We assume here that whether we are talking about automobiles or human beings we are in good running condition!)

If we decide upon an action at this level, it can continue as a benign action, meaning that it will provide positive results for us or for someone else. If we do not consciously call our attention or anyone else's to this fine action of ours, our deed is praiseworthy. Depending upon the good deed, it can be very positive in its results or just so-so. Of course, if we decide to advertise our praiseworthiness to all who would listen, then such an action would have immediate negative results, since few people like to hear others brag about their good deeds. It is very easy for what is praiseworthy to become blameworthy in the eyes of others. On the other hand, if we confess our good deed to our best friend or our husband or wife and our motivation is not pride but the happiness of having learned or gained something of value from the exchange, then we become another exception to the rule, and we might even set a precedent for ourselves. That is, we discovered that one good behaviour was rewarded by another; otherwise, we might never perform that particular good deed again. However, we have also learned that good actions do not always result in further good actions. Whether we wish to admit it or not, our behaviour is modified by rewards and punishments. Unfortunately, we can never know in advance for certain whether an action will result in a plus or a minus experience, or if the outcome of a plus experience will be minus, or if a minus experience will produce a plus result.

The Sliding Scale of Love/Hate

The second example in the diagram, the paired opposites of love and hate, will also provide us with a new insight into that most important of all qualities. Although we have stated that hate is the absence or lack of love, we should refrain from completing this thought with syllogistic logic and conclude, therefore, that hate does not exist. Love and hate are expressions of one quality only; if this most powerful of all emotions cannot express itself ideally in its positive range as the virtue of love, its energy will be manifested in its negative mode, the vice of hate. In its more neutral range, it hovers at a low intensity we call simply 'liking', but at the same time seeking a specific person or object worthy of its fuller power. Sometimes this strongest of all emotions surges and seems to overflow into both its positive and negative modes simultaneously, producing that strange confusion we call a love/hate relationship.

It is important to point out that qualities and emotions are not necessarily interchangeable and cannot always be equated. Certain qualities or conditions can produce pleasant or unpleasant responses that prefer an intellectual outlet, rather than an emotional one. However for the sake of simplifying our explanation, we will consider some qualities, such as love and hate, as equivalent to the emotions they engender. As we think about our own ranges for love and hate, we wonder if everyone expresses this quality as an emotion in identical degrees of intensity. But this is not the case. Although we have no instruments for measuring positive and negative ranges for emotions, we know that some individuals experience life more intensely than others. We can use as examples two married couples who are divorcing.

The first couple experience great trauma from a marriage that was based on deep feelings and emotion. Now they have become two people who are bitter and hateful to each other and are completely devastated by divorce. The second couple, on the other hand, part 'the best of friends'. Their emotional experience seems to leave fewer scars.

Before we applaud this second couple for being more mature

and emotionally stable, we should look further into the dynamics of their life together. We might discover several possibilities that would explain their lesser stress. One possibility is that this couple preferred to respond to people and life as an intellectual experience rather than an emotional one. Their love for each other, while emotional, was constantly being proved and tested as 'two minds' in communication rather than 'two hearts'. We might measure their love as a +5, i.e., they like each other very much. Eventually their bond was not strong enough to keep them together. Or the case might exemplify a couple who at the beginning of their marriage could measure their love as a +8 but – with the passage of time and many unpleasant life experiences together – whose emotional base for a deep love has disintegrated by the time they agree to divorce. In both cases, the emotional investment of an intense love has either decreased or was never really there so that it is possible for them to separate without intense feelings.

Assigning the Intensity Range

What emerges as the most interesting phenomenon in all the above examples is that whatever the degree of intensity experienced as the emotion of a quality in its positive range can be experienced to the same degree of intensity in its negative range. This seems to explain the adage of how some of the greatest saints in the world could have been at one time the greatest sinners.

Intense emotion is intense energy; rather than dissipating, it manifests itself along a bi-polar continuum. We become aware of the entropic effect as we grow older and find that the intensity of our emotional energy seems to decreasse with age. It is also possible for a deeply felt emotion to lessen naturally over a period of time only to re-emerge as added-on energy to another existing quality. Emotional energy not used is redirected.

We can examine the qualities which we call our weaknesses or faults as values occurring in the negative range of our continuum and mentally assign to them the minus value we think they deserve; then we slide our gauge to the same value on the plus side of the scale. Thus, the fault of selfishness can become the virtue of generosity; insensitivity to others can be changed into consideration, self-righteousness into humility, impatience into patience and deceit into honesty. To show just how closely aligned our faults and virtues are to each other, consider the habitual liar who has the uncanny ability to know when someone else is either lying or telling the truth. The reason for this is that the liar himself has the same potential capacity for telling the truth, so he is not easily fooled. The reverse is also true. The one who usually tells the truth can also tell when someone is either lying or telling the truth, for he, too, has this same potential range for this quality as does the liar. The individuals who are fooled the most often are those who sometimes lie and sometimes tell the truth; they mistakenly assume everyone else does the same.

Pairing Opposites

Human beings are also born with certain innate capacities that express particular skills and talents which may be inherited or acquired. These capacities, which vary from individual to individual, are exhibited as part of our 'doing' nature, rather than our 'feeling' nature, and are not qualities that can be expressed along a positive/negative continuum. Pairing opposites correctly is an excursion into the unexplored territory of our inner map.

One of our first mistakes will be to name a secondary emotional response as a primary quality and attempt to pair it with another primary opposite. A good example of this is the emotion we call 'irritability', a condition which describes a kind of negative frustration that causes us to be short-tempered. Irritability has no true opposite because it is not a primary quality. It is a negative secondary emotional response caused either by resentment or by impatience, both primary qualities. Therefore, the proper qualities to be paired are either patience/impatience or acceptance/resentment. If we wish to rid ourselves of our irritability and frustration we must discover what, or who, it is that makes us impatient or resentful and remove its cause. An added bonus accrues because patience and acceptance are neutral benign states that use little energy so what was wasted in our irritated condition is now available for more constructive use.

Occasionally we discover that conventional wisdom has paired

THE UNITY OF OPPOSITES

opposites that do not really match. For example, when we experience fear we assume that its opposite is courage. Even though overcoming fear might make us more courageous, cowardice is the correct opposite of courage. In one of His prayers Bahá'u'lláh talks about changing fear into tranquillity; this makes more sense, for if we overcame all our fears, we would indeed be tranquil. Instincts have no true opposites; the natural instinct of fear protects us by overriding all other inner states, thus triggering the appropriate response that will counteract or remedy a dangerous or stressful situation. Fear – we call its extreme arousal panic – also produces the prime emotion of anxiety, and it is this quality which, when it disappears, moves into its opposite or positive range, tranquillity.

The emotional display of anger is also instinctive, even though it arises as a secondary response to a thwarted desire or an inability to control a particular person, situation or environment. Sustained anger that cannot or will not identify its object will generate such an intense feeling within us that it can make us ill or lead us to violence.

Responses to our instincts can be called forth from conditions existing either outside us or within us. If they arise from vague and unpleasant inner conditions we have not sorted out, they remain as artificial emotional constructs that cause us to experience formless fears and desires, often leading to some undefined anger. When this occurs, we can be certain that we have been incorrectly receiving and interpreting signals that define our reality-base. These psychological distortions of outer and inner reality cause most of our neuroses and psychoses.

A different kind of problem arises from the inadequacies of the English language and the vocabulary it provides. For example, we want to know the opposite of 'compassion'. We may describe it as 'hard-heartedness' but that is not really a quality. We can only speak about a lack of compassion. In this case, compassion is a true quality for which there is no English word to describe its opposite. Fortunately, English allows for common usage to add prefixes such as 'in', or 'non' to designate the lack of something.

Even if we are not too successful in (1) identifying all our weaknesses and faults, or (2) pairing the correct opposites so that we can work on changing our weaknesses into our strengths, resulting in (3) less progress for self-transformation, we will have made progress in a new method of self-examination and self-knowledge.

Adam and Eve and Human Behaviour

Taking our cue from the Bahá'í teachings on the nature of the unity of opposites and how it affects human psychology, we discover yet another dimension to the positive/negative continuum. 'Abdu'l-Bahá provides the framework for this idea in the following explanation of the symbolism of Adam and Eve.

> . . . Adam signifies the heavenly spirit of Adam, and Eve his human soul . . . The tree of good and evil signifies the human world; for the spiritual and divine world is purely good and absolutely luminous, but in the human world light and darkness, good and evil, exist as opposite conditions.[7]
>
> . . . the serpent is that attachment to this world which constitutes sin, and which has infected the descendants of Adam. Christ by His holy breezes saved men from this attachment and freed them from this sin. The sin in Adam is relative to his position. Although from this attachment there proceed results, nevertheless, attachment to the earthly world, in relation to attachment to the spiritual world, is considered as a sin . . . So bodily power is not only defective in relation to spiritual power, it is weakness in comparison. In the same way, physical life, in comparison with eternal life in the Kingdom, is considered as death.[8]

Ancient myths throughout the world relate stories of the 'first man and first woman' and their symbolism is rich and varied. Adam and Eve hold particular fascination for us in the West because of our biblical heritage. In the above passage 'Abdu'l-Bahá explains only one of the 'mysteries', as He called them, of this allegory. The original usage of the word Adam meant collective man (in Hebrew the word 'Adam' signifies all mankind) and represents the evolutionary moment in geologic time when the human species became conscious of its inner spiritual nature, that is, the awakening of the soul, symbolized by the birth of Eve from Adam.

Our long sojourn in a pure and innocent condition at one with nature is symbolized by our child-like existence in the Garden of Eden. Like the animal's natural paradise, our paradise also depended upon nature to provide for all our needs and wants. In this primeval condition there is not yet a need for the latent higher functions of intellect to manifest themselves nor for the expression of free will or free choice. God is our loving but stern parent who must be obeyed. Adam's spirit and will are completely subordinated to God's Will and Spirit. Mankind, seemingly, is not in need or want for anything. But with the emergence of the recognition of our spiritual identity (gained through our knowledge of the Tree of Life), our psychological and intellectual capacities increase, and we become the masters of all other creatures. The human soul (Eve) becomes more and more attracted and attached to earthly delights and gradually forgets its heavenly origin. Finally, the fully-awakened human spirit becomes consciously and intellectually aware of its power to do either good or evil, symbolized by the Tree of Knowledge.

In our animal-like condition we had survived by listening to our natural instincts. We were not confronted with having to make complex choices based on the perception that good and evil were descriptions of our inner and outer worlds. Adam, signifying spiritual man, is now obliged to choose one action over another; but he can choose wisely only if he has knowledge of *both* the good and evil consequences of his actions. The condition of divine knowledge is no longer understood as a unity; man (Adam) now perceived it in its divided polarities of positive and negative, or more simply, as good and evil. As a result, humanity put itself in bondage to earthly and corporeal existence. This was Adam's sin.

In the Bahá'í religion the real existence or condition for mankind, as descendants of the spiritual Adam, is the reclamation of our original spiritual heritage and the regaining of our attachment to the divine or heavenly spirit based not upon innocence or unreasoned faith, but upon conscious knowledge. Humanity is promised this reclamation when it establishes the legendary Kingdom of God on earth.

Virtues are Unlimited

Another of the many points made in the story of Adam and Eve is that what is purely good or divine is infinite and eternal, since all good originates with God. The reverse of this is that what is earthly and material is finite and impermanent. Virtue, or what

91

we interpret as good, then, has no ending in time; vice, or what we interpret as evil, is space/time-bound. 'All evils', 'Abdu'l-Bahá said, 'return to non-existence.'⁹ Put another way, a virtue or quality expressed in its positive mode can be infinitely expanded, while a vice or a quality expressed in its negative mode has a limited range.

Love, for example, is an infinite quality that can build a bridge from our world into the world of God in our love for God. Hate, on the other hand, must have a material object close by to vent itself upon, and if the hate is not appeased it will eventually turn backward and inward and we ourselves become its target. Negatively expressed qualities, once they reach their most intense value, have nowhere else to go, so, like uncontrollable beasts, they at last turn on us. In the best scenario, they cause our emotional problems, and in the worst, they cause insanity. We can cope with just so much evil or vice in ourselves; overloading leads to a breakdown of normal functioning. On the most fundamental level, what we observe is the process of entropy at work.

Any practice of evil is shallow and therefore easy to commit. All vices, like the shadows they are, have no substance, and to be appreciated each one must be endlessly repeated. We should not wonder why vices (evil) appeal to us when we are young; their gratifications are always immediate and their pleasures are usually experienced physically. They are the loosened appetites of our baser or animal nature that can control us only so long as ignorance of the good is not replaced by knowledge of the good.

If what we call virtues, or those qualities based on the knowledge of our higher nature, have no ending in time, then why do we not see more examples of people who desire to attain, or who have already attained, a virtuous nature? And if there were such people, would this mean that there were individuals who were on their way to attaining perfection? This is a frightening thought for most of us. We have been taught that the only perfect people in this world have been the Manifestations of God, and They occupy a station denied to us. If we think of perfection as an absolute state, then this is true, and we are defeated before we begin. However, if we think of human perfection in this contingent world as being a relative state, then there is hope. The Bahá'í idea of perfection and knowledge and how they are attained will be explored in the next chapter.

A New Model of Human Behaviour

We have learned that the path to virtue or perfection is extremely difficult to find, to follow, or to remain upon because it can only be achieved through spiritual knowledge and disciplined hard work. Many of us find it easier to try to perfect others. Or, given the choice, some of us, like Adam and Eve, will choose the darker path back to our animal condition, the path to nature's 'paradise' of bondage. But the majority of us will choose not to make a choice; we will stand with one foot on each path, sampling a little of what both have to offer. This is not what is meant by the golden mean or the path of moderation, but it is a typical indecisive human choice.

The illustration below shows us the three conditions or natures of man. 'Abdu'l-Bahá also gives us a word-picture of these three natures:

As we have before indicated, this human reality stands between the higher and the lower in man, between the world of the animal and the world of Divinity. When the animal proclivity in man becomes predominant, he sinks even lower than the brute. When the heavenly powers are triumphant in his nature, he becomes the noblest and most superior being in the world of creation. All the imperfections found in the animal are found in man. In him there is antagonism, hatred and selfish struggle for existence; in his nature lurk jealousy, revenge, ferocity, cunning, hypocrisy, greed, injustice and tyranny. So to speak, the reality of man is clad in the outer garment of the animal, the habiliments of the world of nature, the world of darkness, imperfections and unlimited baseness.

On the other hand, we find in him justice, sincerity, faithfulness, knowledge, wisdom, illumination, mercy and pity, coupled with intellect, comprehension, the power to grasp the realities of things and the ability to penetrate the truths of existence. All these great perfections are to be found in man. Therefore, we say that man is a reality which stands between light and darkness. From this standpoint his nature is threefold: animal, human and divine. The animal nature is darkness; the heavenly is light in light.[10]

WORLD OF NATURE	WORLD OF MAN	WORLD OF GOD
ANIMAL	**HUMAN**	**SPIRITUAL**

FREE CHOICE

Darkness → Illumination

Ignorance → Understanding

Evil → Good

Vice → Virtue

Imperfections → Perfections

Hate → Love

Unresolved Conflict	Direction
Confusion	Challenges
Distortion	Values
Neurosis	
Crime	
Insanity	Personality Unification

DISFUNCTION	**CONFORMITY**	**CREATIVITY**

'Man stands at the end of night and the beginning of day.'

'Abdu'l-Bahá

The human spirit or soul becomes either degraded or uplifted as we make our experiential choices. 'Abdu'l-Bahá said that to stand still is to move backwards. In the spiritual world all motion is forward; lack of spiritual progress is atrophic, leading to spiritual 'death'. In another interesting observation of the human condition 'Abdu'l-Bahá pointed out that

> Just as the earth attracts everything to the centre of gravity and every object thrown upward into space will come down, so also material ideas and worldly thoughts attract man to the centre of self. Anger, passion, ignorance, prejudice, greed, envy, covetousness, jealousy and suspicion prevent man from ascending to the Realms of Holiness, imprisoning him in the claws of self and the jail of egotism. The physical man, unassisted by divine power, trying to escape from one of these invisible enemies, will fall unconsciously into the hands of another. No sooner does he attempt to soar upward than the density of the love of self, like the power of gravity, draws him to the earth. But the only power that is capable of delivering man from this captivity is the power of the breaths of the Holy Spirit.[11]

If what some psychologists call the subconscious mind, or the 'id', is really the workings of our 'old brain', then it is a powerful reminder of our primitive and animalistic side. It is the seat of our instincts and emotions. If we ignore, suppress, avoid or attempt to control our instincts and the emotions they engender, then, like the body's immunological system gone haywire, they will react as a constantly 'turned on' warning system which will eventually attack its host with destructive consequences.

Any wilful, destructive act we commit must be admitted and confronted so that we can change our responses. Our evils, real or imagined, are nothing but our own inner weaknesses and insecurities that we developed and nurtured as survival mechanisms first as infants, then as children and adolescents. They are the immature expressions of our basic emotional instincts that we no longer need to indulge.

A new kind of psychology is needed to deal with all three conditions of our nature with a new breed of wise psychologists who can take us from the paths of self-destruction into the light of mature self-realization, and admit to the spiritual part of our species. Insight into self and self-discovery oftentimes needs the help of such experts; others make headway on their own. Self-knowledge is the prerequisite to self-transformation, a truth every Messenger of God has stressed.

How to Change Negative Qualities into their Opposites

The kind of self-transformation the Divine Revelators talk about comes from the understanding and application of Their teachings. These form the foundation for all lasting changes of behaviour. These teachings, however, do not provide us with a simplistic checklist of obvious truisms to repair our damaged psyches. There are no magical phrases or formulas to be repeated, nor is there such a thing as a 'quick spiritual fix' gained through the use of drugs. If we want spiritual trans-formation we must work on changing what is negative in us into its opposite.

If we think about the fear and desire motivations that are so deeply ingrained within us, it would seem to be a hopeless task to change or eliminate them; but there is a spiritual solution. The Holy Prophets supplied the answer when They told us to fear God, and that by doing so we exchange all of our material and psychological fears for only one fear which we put into God's hands. They also taught us to modify the outlets for our over-powering material wants and desires by being motivated by the basic spiritual desire to know and to love God. Both instincts, now being centred and focused on the highest of spiritual goals, gradually eliminate those misdirected worldly and personal targets which cause our problems.

In addition, the Holy Teachers tell us how important it is that we learn how to pray sincerely for those changes. Prayer is a power that always comes as a surprise to those who use it for the first time. Most of us have never learned how to pray; repeating words that demand from God that which we have already made up our minds we need or want, is not prayer. Both Bahá'u'lláh and 'Abdu'l-Bahá have revealed prayers that implore God's aid in changing our weaknesses into strengths. Little by little we learn not to command God to rid us of our irritations in life but, rather, to instil in us a pure heart and a tranquil conscience. We ask Him to guide us, to instruct us and to provide the means for our growth.

In order to know if a weakness has been reversed, it is

necessary to recognize when we have acquired its opposite, its strength. In the quotation that opens this chapter, 'Abdu'l-Bahá states that we cannot know perfection, virtue or knowledge in ourselves unless we define and compare them to their lack or decrease. He does not tell us that it is necessary or essential to experience vice, ignorance and imperfection, or those qualities we call evil, but that we must know and understand what they are. Also, He does not say we are irretrievably lost if we have already committed evil acts. What is necessary is that, like the Zoroastrians, we do battle with our demons and our satans, and make every effort to win. The Bahá'í philosopher Horace Holley wrote about this inner battle in the following passage:

> In this clear, unflickering light reflected from the mind of 'Abdu'l-Bahá as from a burnished mirror held to the sun, humanity has been granted capacity of vision in the otherwise darkened subjective world. By His insight one can rise above the mass consciousness and apprehend the meaning of the age not as the superficial clash of nations, classes and races, but as the final struggle of the animal nature with the spiritual nature of man. The raging tornado has its central point of perfect calm, and the Faith of Bahá'u'lláh promulgated by 'Abdu'l-Bahá is the universal peace hidden from physical sight behind the desperate movements of the dying civilization in which we live.[12]

The biblical final battle of Armageddon turns out not to be a war fought between nations but a spiritual battle fought inside ourselves. It is not waiting to be fought; it is upon us, and we have been engaged in this battle for some time.

7

Knowledge and Perfection:
Little by Little, Degree by Degree

. . . as long as man is in the matrix of the human world, as long as he is the captive of nature, he is out of touch and without knowledge of the universe of the Kingdom. If he attains rebirth while in the world of nature, he will become informed of the divine world. He will observe that another and a higher world exists. Wonderful bounties descend; eternal life awaits . . . All the signs of reality and greatness are there. He will see the lights of God . . . for the perfect man there are two kinds of birth: the first, physical birth, is from the matrix of the mother; the second, or spiritual birth, is from the world of nature. In both he is without knowledge of the new world of existence he is entering. Therefore, rebirth means his release from the captivity of nature, freedom from attachment to this mortal and material life.[1]

The greatest gifts of man are reason and eloquence of expression. The perfect man is both intelligent and eloquent. He has knowledge, and knows how to express it. Unless man express himself in this day, he will remain like a closed casket, and one cannot know whether it contains jewels or glass.[2]

Does Language Precede Knowledge?

By the middle of this century the majority of the contemporary schools of philosophy were arguing that knowledge is only a construct of language and that it is language that gives coherency to the universe and to our lives. They say that

98

everything we think and do can be traced back to a shared and accepted discourse that verbally describes what we call reality. With this argument the knower and the known are not two things, but one. Not only is knowledge reduced to each person's subjective understanding of how to use language, but this line of reasoning eliminates knowledge as a real category. (If this is true, we might slyly interject at this point the question, how can these philosophers *know* this?) It is inarguable that language has become inseparable from knowledge in many ways, but it seems illogical to infer from this that we must first seek language and then invent knowledge to justify it. If this were the case, we could not explain how knowledge of this idea preceded our carrying it out.

The Bahá'í definition of true knowledge – that it is the accumulation of our understanding of what is Real based upon the teachings of the Divine Prophets – suggests that this authentic knowledge exists as part of the order of the universe. This spiritual definition distinguishes knowledge as something intelligible because the universe itself is intelligible. Its comprehension can be organized into coherency by means of an intelligible language system. Everything in the universe 'communicates' on one level or another, but can all communication be called a 'language'? If language is defined by the social agreement of specified rules for words and symbols that must be learned, then parrots and computers are no different from us. Communication, on the other hand, is spontaneous and innate, and can take many different forms of expression. The missing element that must be introduced here is that of comprehension; without it, a spoken or written language is gibberish. We argue that human beings are knowers first, speakers second.

History as Cyclical and Linear Time

Linguists have noted that the particular language system a culture invents or adopts will significantly structure the way its members think about things. How a culture decides to conceptualize and talk about time, for example, will be more crucial to its future than how it perceives objects in space. Cultures and civilizations must be future-oriented if they are to progress.

There are basically two conceptually different ways a culture's language describes time. Various words have been used by scholars in related disciplines to describe these patterns of time, but for our purposes the simple terms 'cyclical' and 'linear' will be used to illustrate how a culture senses time as historic time, or the *long view* of time. The most important determinant for how a particular civilization views historic time can be traced to its dominant religious philosophies. We have come to see the Eastern or Hindu–Buddhist way as being a cyclical view, while the Judaic–Christian–Islamic view is predominantly linear. We will examine briefly a few of the more important perceptions that result from these two views and how they affect the general way populations assess knowledge.

History seen as cyclical time means that both beginnings and endings of events are somewhat vague; what is important is what happens in between. Major themes are the repetition of events, the return of consequences and the inevitability of karma. Subjective and immediate concerns of people are more likely to take precedence over remote events.

History associated with the linear point of view sees events in time as having both beginnings and endings, and includes such major themes as events pointing both to a direction and a goal. History is seen as evolutionary with some higher purpose as the end result. Events and life are viewed from a distance, with time being irreversible.

We can immediately identify with one or the other view, depending on which culture we were born into. Each provides a wide base of knowledge that a civilization unconsciously adopts. These generalized orientations to knowledge result from how each society understands its respective scriptures and how these scriptures depict history's past and future. Neither view by itself, however, represents a true picture either of history or of time as taught by the Messengers of God, for elements of both paradigms are found in each of Their teachings. The bias occurs because we tend to read only one side of the page, so to speak, and not the other.

Cyclical time entraps us slowly in circles of repetition and return, resulting in the notion of the reincarnation of the human soul. Conversely, linear time rushes by us and its forward inevitability can fill us with apprehension. On the one hand, the possibility that time and the world might end horrifies us, while our lack of living up to God's, or our own, expectations only adds to our burdens. With either scenario, losing seems to occur more frequently than winning. But of the two interpretations, it is the linear point of view which ultimately holds the most hope. It offers mankind a direction for the future, as well as a purpose and a goal. Each tomorrow offers the possibility of things hoped-for or promised, and the probability of change.

The Bahá'í Epistemology

Bahá'u'lláh resolves the ancient question of whether knowledge (or ideas) is innate by pointing out that knowledge is not a 'something' we come equipped with at birth, that ideas are not immaculately conceived, despite the arguments of Plato. He tells us that only the Manifestations of God have innate knowledge. As human beings, however, we do come equipped with minds and intellects which innately desire information of the whys, hows and whats of our existence. For the answers we look to our scientists and philosophers, our religious leaders and our governments, all of whom speak to us in our own familiar language. But when 'Abdu'l-Bahá spoke to American audiences in the year 1912 he shattered many of our notions as to where and in whom we can place our reliance to provide true knowledge. He said there are four general ways people arrive at knowledge of things, and all of them are imperfect and incomplete.

The first method is through our sense perceptions. With this method we rely upon our own experiences, observations, and subjective as well as objective testing. Although this method is the most direct and immediate, and we share this method with animals as well, it is not the most accurate. As a way to knowledge, there is not a human being on earth who does not use it and rely on it for most of his first-hand knowledge of the world. Its inductions yield practical and common-sense information. The empirical school of philosophy considered it to be the only validation of knowledge. Our technologies and applied sciences are the direct outcome of this kind of pragmatism. This is the path of observing and assessing what is evident in our environment. In the hands of trained scientists and their instruments it has produced remarkable results. For the rest of us, if we rely only upon our senses to give us accuracy, proof and truth at all times and under all conditions, it will lead us to errors. What our eyes see and what is really there can result in distorted objectivity as our imaginations incorrectly interpret what we think we see. 'In brief, the senses are continually deceived, and we are unable to separate that which is reality from that which is not.'[3]

The second criterion for establishing knowledge is through our intellect or reason. This method relies on the tool of logic and consistency of thought to provide accurate explanations of the world around us. The method itself is one of reasonable interpretation based on logical and critical analysis. Although most individuals who use this method would be the first to admit that it is not infallible, they will insist that it is the *right* method. As a bare bones statement, this is probably true; ultimately all our statements of truth are weighed in the balance of reason. The problem lies in the proliferation of differing bases of knowledge in every discipline and field of endeavour which are continually shifting and changing. All of these foundations of knowledge have been based on reason and logic. Unfortunately, each of their premises for truth has been founded upon differing points of view so their conclusions seldom agree. What they lack is an accepted common framework of theoretical truth which would unify all their approaches. 'Abdu'l-Bahá states that reason and logic by themselves will not point the way to true knowledge. '. . . nothing is fixed, nothing final; everything is continually changing because human reason is progressing along new roads of investigation and arriving at new conclusions every day. In the future much that is announced and accepted as true now will be rejected and disproved.'[4]

The third criterion is knowledge preserved as traditions – those standards of cultural acceptance that come to us through institutionalized religions and their spokesmen. Kingdoms and empires have arisen and fallen because of their insistence upon the rightness of a particular religious belief system. Various doctrines and dogma have been more instrumental in shaping our standards for assessing knowledge and truth than both philosophy and science combined. Why should this be so? We are told that scripture is the word of God and so it must be believed. But 'Abdu'l-Bahá tells us this cannot be resolved quite so simply:

For religious traditions are the report and record of understanding and interpretation of the Book. By what means has this understanding, this interpretation been reached? By the analysis of human reason. When we read the Book of God, the faculty of comprehension by which we form conclusions is reason. Reason is mind. If we are not endowed with perfect reason, how can we comprehend the meaning of the Word of God? Therefore, human reason, as already pointed out, is by its very nature finite and faulty in conclusions. It cannot surround the Reality Itself, the Infinite Word. Inasmuch as the source of traditions and interpretations is human reason, and human reason is faulty, how can we depend upon its findings for real knowledge?[5]

'Abdu'l-Bahá does not say that we must eschew reason and logic when we read the holy books; He only reminds us that those who speak with authority use their own reason and logic to interpret scripture and have thereby created any number of conflicting interpretations as to the correct meaning of the word of God. Both the second and third ways of knowing make language inseparable from knowledge.

The fourth methodology for determining knowledge is what we call inspiration. This is a method of direct and personal 'revelation', similar to intuitive or insight learning. Although the majority of us agree that inspiration and intuition exist as inner states, we are not quite sure where they come from. Nonetheless, there are those individuals who swear that their intuition is infallible and who are certain that God has personally singled them out to be His channel. Those who feel personally inspired are just as certain that God has chosen them for this gift. 'Abdu'l-Bahá says that it is the human spirit which generates these bursts of creative thought and feelings, and, of course, all of us possess these powers to one degree or another. 'How shall we know whether we are following inspiration from God or satanic promptings of the human soul?'[6] An inspiration for action for one person may be just a daydream for another. Whenever we compare ideas or thoughts based on intuition or inspiration we find that the conclusions reached vary considerably. Our intuitive promptings and our creative inspirations are filtered through our intellect and interpreted by our emotions in a creative but very subjective process.

The Degrees of Knowledge

Another way we can orient ourselves to knowledge is to look at it the way the Messengers of God have taught it. They provide the divine path to knowledge. We can categorize this generally as: 1) man's knowledge of man, 2) man's knowledge of the Divine, 3) God's knowledge of man and 4) God's knowledge of Himself. This model depicts knowledge as possessing a similar hierarchic nature as in our description of Reality/reality. We will survey these four levels of knowledge to see what new things they have to tell us.

In the first level exists all of man's accumulated knowledge of himself and his world. It is the knowledge we learned as children at home and later in school. Most of it is empirical and pragmatic knowledge; it yields primarily accessible information, that is, information that our particular culture has accepted as 'facts'. It is relative knowledge gained by the four methodologies mentioned by 'Abdu'l-Bahá. Since it is based upon innumerable perceptions and preconceptions of how things are and should be, this factual knowledge will be true only so long as its conditions remain constant. In its more objective and scholarly form it is concerned with the relationships of things and how they affect each other.

These accumulated pieces of knowledge represent what mankind has learned about himself and his world that have withstood the tests of time. Each piece can be compared to a letter or a word of an infinite alphabet or glossary that we arrange and rearrange until we get a meaningful ideational combination. Certain letters and words link up with other letters and words, and some combinations with other combinations. Many are thought-provoking, complex and even elegant combinations. Many have gained a respected place and have been proved to be true, but most of them float and shift and change from one relative position to another. Knowledge on this level is a moving and dynamic world of observation, thought and application, and we often become enamoured by its kaleidoscopic nature. Individuals who emerge from educational institutions on the higher levels will readily recognize that their academic experience consisted of identifying and memorizing particular groupings of information in order to determine why certain combinations of 'facts' fit together and what their interactions might mean.

Occasionally, one of the pieces or combinations of knowledge points to an idea not covered by the information contained within this level. The curious scholar is then confronted with missing pieces from the puzzle that he or she must find in order to complete the picture. What has happened is this: a door has been opened into another world, the world of the second level of knowledge which we have named man's glimpse into the Divine Realm.

This level of understanding can tell us things about our very deepest natures as well as revealing the innermost secrets of the universe. In this realm they seem somehow to be connected. It is the world that can be unlocked by religion, theoretical physics and the fine arts, revealing knowledge outside the scope of man's everyday observation and manipulation. It seems to be a world whose laws and principles manipulate us and which lies beyond our tinkering.

This level contains no isolated numbers or letters or pieces of knowledge. The fragmented knowledge of 'facts' has been subsumed by larger systems of a more abstract nature. If our understanding can encompass these larger collections, it will automatically include the understanding of their smaller components. Comprehension of this type is not only more efficient, but it is a faster and more innovative way of knowing, as Ludwig von Bertalanffy's General System Theory (see Chapter Ten) set out to prove and which the mythical Circadians also discovered. This orientation enables us to see into corners of our world we were unable to see before. Problems can be solved that previously escaped us by allowing us to use the more inclusive equation, principle or law. By using the larger principle or generality we are also able to discern more readily what constitutes true knowledge and what does not, for the truths of the lower level are determined by the laws and principles of the encompassing one. In the Bahá'í Faith this method is used by the members of their deliberating bodies in a process called 'consultation' that enables them to search out the truth of a matter before reaching a solution.

But even in this rarefied atmosphere we realize how limited our capacity is for attaining any final truth. We come to the realization that what is possible to know is truly infinite, and that even the knowledge contained within each structured stratum is unlimited. Bahá'u'lláh poetically described this level of knowledge: 'In the ocean he findeth a drop, in a drop he beholdeth the secrets of the sea.'[7]

If we could cross the boundary into the third plane to encompass God's knowledge of His creation, we would see that the collections of knowledge have become even more rarefied. Here, we might refer to merging clusters of knowledge, where knowledge can be known 'all at once' in its entirety. It would be akin to being able to see simultaneously both white light and the full spectral display of its colours. Here, separated knowledge would be seen to be an illusion; on this level exists the true knowledge of Reality, unified and undivided. If we could imagine the mind of a Messenger of God, it would be in this world that it would operate. Bahá'u'lláh speaks of this last degree of knowledge possible to human attainment as the condition where the end and the beginning are one: '. . . nay, they see neither beginning nor end, and witness neither "first" nor "last" . . . For these have passed over the worlds of names, and fled beyond the worlds of attributes as swift as lightning . . . And they have made their dwelling-place in the shadow of the Essence.'[8] This station of knowledge is seldom attained by mortals in this life but only glimpsed in the mirror of Reality held before us by our Holy Prophets.

The last and ultimate degree of knowledge is God's knowledge of Himself. This is absolute knowledge and the source of all other knowledge. It is unknown and unknowable, beyond language and beyond thought. It is God's final mystery wrapped within Himself.

The Unification of Knowledge

Creative inspiration, discovery and inventiveness may very well be the results of sudden and partial flashes of awareness and insight into these higher realms of knowledge, the 'gift of the Holy Spirit'. Each degree of true knowledge contains its own secrets and delights which are revealed to us when we open ourselves to their bestowals.

'Abdu'l-Bahá has stated that knowledge on the first level is available to us all, for it is mostly our own invention. What we understand of it has been gained through our own powers and by our own choices. But to attain knowledge on the higher levels we must open our inner eyes and ears and commit ourselves to finding truth. 'Abdu'l-Bahá summarizes the place of the intellect and the spirit in comprehending the higher degrees of knowledge in these words:

> He has bestowed upon him the power of intellect so that through the attribute of reason, when fortified by the Holy Spirit, he may penetrate and discover ideal realities and become informed of the mysteries of the world of significances. As this power to penetrate the ideal knowledges is super-human, supernatural, man becomes the collective centre of spiritual as well as material forces so that the divine spirit may manifest itself in his being . . . and the mysteries of the realm of might be unsealed.[9]

Comparisons are Relative

To most of us the word 'perfection' is yet another word that designates an either-or state. We have come to believe that something is either perfect or it is not. But a careful reading of a dictionary definition tells us that this is not the case. Perfection is defined as completion, full development, faultlessness and comparative excellence. Nothing can be completed or arrive at full development or faultlessness unless it has undergone a perfecting process. Each later stage is always compared to its previous stage or the one to follow. There is obviously no way of knowing what is best, unless we know first what is better. There will always be one more perfect sunset, one more perfect bloom and one more perfect melody. Of course, we will never be able to compare the final or absolute state of perfection of anything since we have no idea of what that might be.

How Do We Account for an Imperfect World?

The argument might be raised that the idea of perfection is just another illusion and that we have all been tricked into believing that a loving and perfect Creator watches over us in this 'best of all possible worlds'. When we look around us and consider the misery and suffering of our planet's multitudes over successive centuries of history, we are tempted to agree with Voltaire's cynical assessment not only of perfection but also of God and the world. We, too, have observed nature through countless centuries and watched helplessly as she unleashed earthquakes, hurri-canes and other disasters wreaking their devastation. At the same time we have wondered why we allow ourselves to become the victims of our own calamities, such as ruinous wars, raging injustices and other acts of cruelty too numerous to name. Where, then, is God's perfection in either nature or man?

Chapter Six argued that evil is ignorance and imperfection, while the attainment of ideal characteristics is both our wisdom and our perfection. This argument, however, cannot be applied to explain the natural forces and energies of this planet when they seem to be destructive, so we must conclude that nature has nothing to do with our invented concepts of good and evil. Earth, as a living planet, acts in accordance with those universal divine laws which dictate her survival and thereby our own. 'Abdu'l-Bahá spoke of the inherent perfection of all things created by God:

> For all existing beings ... as well as this limitless space and all that is in it, have been created and organized, composed, arranged, and perfected as they ought to be; the universe has no imperfection, so that if all beings became pure intelligence and reflected for ever and ever, it is impossible that they could imagine anything better than that which exists.
>
> If, however, the creation in the past had not been adorned with utmost perfection, then existence would have been imperfect and meaningless, and in this case creation would have been incomplete. The question needs to be considered with the greatest attention and thought.[10]

To believe in an imperfect universe is to argue that an omniscient God, the source of all perfection, makes mistakes and absent-mindedly fashions a defective universe. Original imperfection is impossible because an imperfect universe would soon have destroyed itself.

> There is another more subtle proof: all these endless beings which inhabit the world, whether man, animal, vegetable, mineral – whatever they may be – are surely, each one of them, composed of elements. There is no doubt that this perfection which is in all beings is caused by the creation of God from the composing elements ... For all beings are connected together like a chain; and reciprocal help, assistance and interaction belonging to the properties of things are the causes of the existence, development and growth of created beings ... Finally, the perfection of each individual being –

that is to say, the perfection which you now see in man or apart from him, with regard to their atoms, members or powers – is due to the composition of the elements, to their measure, to their balance, to the mode of their combination, and to mutual influence.[11]

This kind of elemental perfection is seen in its most awesome demonstrations by nuclear physicists. When these scientists attempt to describe or explain this sub-atomic world they often sound like poets or mystics. If imperfection does not exist naturally on this most fundamental level, then it cannot exist naturally on any level. What we see as imperfection in our world is not the essence of any composed object but rather its acquired characteristics. When we speak about imperfection we are usually speaking about purely human traits or of things familiar to our own personalized world.

Standards of Perfection

Social and religious standards for judging relative perfection now fluctuate almost from decade to decade. Perfections in the human world primarily describe physical beauty and artistic talents. We seldom talk about perfect minds or perfect emotions. We have a peculiar way of assessing other inner qualities; if someone is very kind, surely a virtue or perfection, we say such a one is kind *to a fault*! For the majority of people, acquiring ideal attributes or perfecting one's character ceased to be a common or popular goal when the various 'immediate' media invaded our lives in the middle of this century. Even religious salvation has taken on the form of a simple recipe easily attainable by everyone. If the more cynical among us dismiss the perfecting process on the grounds that it is either impossible, boring or that it requires too much effort, they have either ignored or misunderstood both the process and the goal.

Bahíyyih Khánum, one of Bahá'u'lláh's daughters who lived well into this century, is a good example of a person who attained her true spiritual identity and acquired inner perfections. She accompanied her Father and His family on His exiles and imprisonments, was severely deprived of most material comforts, experienced both physical and psychological stresses throughout her life, as did her brother 'Abdu'l-Bahá, and yet she emerged as one of the most remarkable women of this or any century. She was described by an early American believer on pilgrimage in the Holy Land as one who had been crucified and resurrected in another world. On her passing, another Western Bahá'í paid this tribute to her, a tribute which portrays her great strength of character and her capacious, all-embracing wisdom concerning people and life:

> Something greater than forgiveness she had shown in meeting the cruelties and strictures in her own life. To be hurt and to forgive is saintly but far beyond this is the power to comprehend and not be hurt. This power she had . . . acceptance without complaint has come to be associated with her name. She was never known to complain or lament. It is not that she made the best of things, but that she found in everything, even in calamity itself, the germs of enduring wisdom. She did not resist the shocks and upheavals of life and she did not run counter to obstacles. She was never impatient. She was as incapable of impatience as she was of revolt. But this was not so much long-sufferance as it was quiet awareness of the forces that operate in the hours of waiting and inactivity.
>
> Always she moved with the larger rhythm, the wider sweep, toward the ultimate goal. Surely, confidently, she followed the circle of her orbit round the Sun of her existence, in that complete acquiescence, that perfect accord, which underlies faith itself.[12]

Humanity has a way of making God its scapegoat and blaming Him for the horrors and mistakes it refuses to acknowledge. The Bahá'í teachings make it clear that man's evils and miseries result from his own imperfect decisions based upon his habits of selfishness, ignorance, arrogance and greed. Nations and societies historically make the same kinds of decisions based on those same destructive motivations. The cyclical view of historic time would see these mistakes as being inevitably repeated over and over, with future generations learning nothing from their past. The linear view of historic time would seek to place the blame, and then attempt to rectify each mistake as it was made, one at a time. Neither method encourages a perfecting process.

God, through His Divine Messengers, has repeatedly given humanity spiritual principles with which to solve its problems; what is left up to man is the responsibility to make proper decisions utilizing these principles. When injustices and suffering occur, the ethical framework for their solution has already been provided; what has not been provided is an automated humanity whose members always press the right buttons. As decision-makers, individuals and nations we are as yet imperfect. We have no one but ourselves to blame for the ills that beset us if those misfortunes could have been avoided through having made a better choice. If we habitually avoid the larger wisdom in favour of the lesser or shorter term answer, then both collective man and individual man must accept the consequences. What this means is that we continually and deliberately reinforce imperfect behaviours rather than opting for opportunities to perfect human behaviour and thereby civilization. We, as individual beings, are constantly being replaced on this earth, so our wrong choices can be corrected or remedied more easily by others after we are gone than can the wrong choices nations make.

Whether governments wage war or peace, destroy civilizations or create them, or whether they opt to leave an intellectual and spiritual legacy to their descendants has become the most important concern for us as individuals to address. For those leaders in government and those instrumental in shaping world opinion, the seeking of solutions to mankind's problems based on spiritual and divine law is the greatest moral imperative facing civilization as this century draws to a close.

> Nothing has been created without a special destiny, for every creature has an innate degree of perfection to which he must attain . . . In each kingdom of nature there are potentialities, and each must be cultivated in order to attain its fulfilment. The divine teachers desire man to be educated, that he may attain to the high rank of his own reality . . . The flower needs light in order to attain to its heritage, man needs the light of the holy spirit, and the difference of illumination necessary throughout creation is proportionate with the different kingdoms.
>
> When we come to the estate of man, we find his kingdom is vested with a divine superiority. Compared to the animal, his perfection or his imperfection is superior. In comparison with man, the perfection of a flower is insignificant.[13]

Little by Little, Degree by Degree

Individuals, like nations, do not willingly choose the perfecting process without misgivings. Like the attainment of knowledge, perfection is gained little by little, degree by degree, in small doses that enable us to digest and assimilate what we have learned and what we have become. This is not a painless process for, once begun, it forces us to sacrifice certain behavioural attitudes and patterns that we have spent years developing. To become once more 'pure in heart', great strength of spirit and strength of character are required, qualities we lacked as innocent children. We have grown accustomed to stumbling along with all our psychological crutches. It is for these reasons that few individuals are able to make much progress in their inner growth, and there are fewer still who are motivated at all to begin this interior journey.

> The aim of the prophet of God is to raise man to the degree of knowledge of his potentiality, and to illuminate him through the light of the kingdom, to transform ignorance into wisdom, injustice into justice, error into knowledge, cruelty into affection and incapability into progress. In short, to make all the attainments of existence resplendent in him.[14]

The important point made here is that relative perfection is not a static condition awaiting our discovery, but is a continual honing process. What is attained is not *one* condition of perfection, but *many* perfections. These are acquired one at a time, perhaps one leading to another. We will never know for certain whether a particular perfection is attained, for the possibility always exists that there is another, higher degree to reach. 'Abdu'l-Bahá affirmed that although human perfections are endless, it is not possible to reach a 'limit of perfection' because then 'one of the realities of the beings might reach the condition of being independent of God'; therefore, 'for every being there is a point which it cannot overpass . . .'[15]

The Ultimate Enclosure

As our wisdom increases, our perfections increase; and as perfections are attained, wisdom is attained. In the third level of knowledge, the realm of God's knowledge of His creation, both knowledge and perfection have merged into one divine attribute.

If the unlimited range of knowledge and human perfections were not possible for us to attain, God would indeed be our own invention, a creator as finite and limited as our own imperfect minds. Yet, no created being or civilization can claim to have reached a final stage of perfection; if such a general condition of perfection occurred, all progress and evolution would cease, and decay and dissolution would begin, for there would be nothing further to challenge or to achieve. Only the Manifestations of God have looked across the human boundaries into the world beyond the planes of limitations. But not even They have crossed the barrier into the Absolute. As long as solving one mystery always leads to another, we know that what we know and what we presently are, are not enough.

8

The Universal Glue

O SON OF MAN!
Veiled in My immemorial being and in the ancient eternity of
My essence, I knew My love for thee; therefore I created thee,
have engraved on thee Mine image and revealed to thee My
beauty.

O SON OF MAN!
I loved thy creation, hence I created thee. Wherefore, do thou
love Me, that I may name thy name and fill thy soul with the
spirit of life.

O SON OF BEING!
Love Me, that I may love thee. If thou lovest Me not, My love
can in no wise reach thee. Know this, O servant.

O SON OF MAN!
If thou lovest Me, turn away from thyself; and if thou seekest
My pleasure, regard not thine own; that thou mayest die in Me
and I may eternally live in thee.

O SON OF BEING!
My love is My stronghold; he that entereth therein is safe and
secure, and he that turneth away shall surely stray and perish.

O SON OF THE WONDROUS VISION!
I have breathed within thee a breath of My own Spirit, that
thou mayest be My lover. Why hast thou forsaken Me and
sought a beloved other than Me?[1]

114

The Nexus of Divine Unity

If the unified energy force which holds the physical universe together were equated with its unified spiritual counterpart, that force would be Love. The spiritual explanation of all the cosmic forces unified as one yields essentially the same universe as the scientific explanation. In that 'beginning which hath no beginning' the Bahá'í religion hypothesizes that the visible universe materialized from one force or energy obeying one law which then generated itself in a myriad of complexities. Its first unfoldment manifested those initial conditions necessary to maintain states of matter that would shift dynamically between randomness and order, equilibrium and disequilibrium. This tension ordains the eventual formation and structure of all matter, allowing its progression from an original simplicity to an increasingly highly-organized complexity, thereby ensuring a universe capable of eternally transforming itself.

This one omnipresent energy/force, which we have called the Divine Spirit of God, was given the name of Love by Christ and it sufficed as His definition of God. Understanding God as Love enabled His followers to understand how God could create man in His image and care for him as in a parent/child relationship.

But comprehending the deeper meanings of what Christ and the Holy Messengers meant by Love is neither so simple nor self-evident. 'Abdu'l-Bahá explained this fundamental law in the following way:

> Matter, reflecting the negative aspect of God, is self sufficient, eternal and fills all space. Spirit, flowing out from God, permeates all matter. This spirit – love – reflecting the positive and active aspect of God, impresses its nature upon the atoms and the elements. By its power they are attracted to each other under certain ordered relations and thus, uniting and continuing to unite, give birth to worlds and to systems of worlds.[2]

In other statements, 'Abdu'l-Bahá equates this spirit of Love with the First Emanation of God; this first law is sometimes called His first principle, the *logos* or His first word. Emanation as law or principle has been much more difficult to grasp than emanation as Love. Whatever we choose to name it, it is the first expression or 'word' of God as He wills creation into being. It is His active aspect moving and energizing the void. This one

115

positive creative emanation has enclosed within it all other physical and spiritual laws affecting energy and matter.

The Divine Spirit is the activated force of God's Love; they are not two realities but one reality. God's Spirit of life does not diffuse aimlessly throughout the cosmos; as divine subject it seeks an object.

The quotation above tells us that inanimate matter is imbued with only the passive aspect of this force in its most basic mode, attraction or gravitation to other matter. Inorganic life cannot actively or consciously choose to return God's love to Him. Nor can simple organic life-forms or even the higher forms of animal life translate or identify this abstraction we call Divine Love. For this realization to occur a conscious 'object' is required that has been created containing both the active and passive aspects of this animating force of Love. Throughout the universe there is only one life-form endowed with this kind of completeness – reasoning spiritual beings who are both consciously desirous and willing to return God's love to Him in order to complete the eternal circle of motion and life. It is the human being, Bahá'u'lláh tells us, for whom God created the universe and eternity.

> Love is the most great law that ruleth this mighty and heavenly cycle, the unique power that bindeth together the divers elements of this material world, the supreme magnetic force that directeth the movements of the spheres in the celestial realms. Love revealeth with unfailing and limitless power the mysteries latent in the universe.[3]

> We declare that love is the cause of the existence of all phenomena and that the absence of love is the cause of disintegration or non-existence ... If love were extinguished ... the phenomena of human life would disappear.[4]

> If this love penetrate the heart of man, all the forces of the universe will be realized in him, for it is a divine power ...[5]

Because God's Love will never cease, motion and life can never cease, and because motion and life will never cease, the process of universal creation is continuous and eternal. It is truly Love that makes the universe go 'round; it is its very pulse and heartbeat.

Another way to connect the force of Love which lies at the

116

heart of all matter with that of the generating power of primordial motion is clarified by 'Abdu'l-Bahá:

> Creation is the expression of motion. Motion is life. A moving object is a living object whereas that which is motionless and inert is as dead. All created forms are progressive in their planes or kingdoms of existence under the stimulus of the power or spirit of life. The universal energy is dynamic. Nothing is stationary in the material world of outer phenomena or in the inner world of intellect and consciousness.[6]

The Four Kinds of Divine Love

The basic message of all the Revelators of God is that there is no power or force in the universe greater than God's Love for His creation. Without it, nothing could long endure; without it our lives would be unbearable and we would spend our time in lonely pursuits leading to personal negation. But as we shall soon see, love is simple, love is complex.

Human love, which is always conditioned, can only be understood in its relation to God's Love, which is always unconditioned. (To distinguish between the two, God's Love will be capitalized.) To help us comprehend unconditioned Love, Bahá'u'lláh offers the following explanation. First we are told that there are four aspects to Divine Love: (1) the Love of God towards His own identity, (2) the Love of God for His creatures, (3) the Love of man for his Creator and (4) the Love of man for man.

The reader will, of course, immediately recognize that this arrangement is identical with the four kinds of divine knowledge. The only difference is that the sequence has been deliberately reversed. In the case of the description of knowledge, it seems obvious that man must first acquire knowledge of himself and things before he attempts to reach up to the knowledge of God, therefore relative knowledge was given as the 'first' type of knowledge. Knowledge has always been easier for us to acquire than any variety of love. For this reason any understanding of Love must begin with God, the basis and source for all other kinds of love.

The first divine state is God's Love for Himself, hidden within His pre-existent being and whose condition is unknowable and eternal. Of it, 'Abdu'l-Bahá said, 'This is the transfiguration of His Beauty, the reflection of Himself in the mirror of His Creation. This is the reality of love, the Ancient Love, the Eternal Love. Through one ray of this Love all other love exists'.[7]

The second type of Divine Love God manifests to His creation, evidenced by all phenomena existing through the motion of His Holy and Divine Spirit. This Love allows each created thing to be able to express and demonstrate its purpose and function in the chain of hierarchic existences. It is through this Love that God raised man in His image.

The third type of Love, the Love of man for God, is possible to attain only through the holy teachings and by loving the Teachers who brought them. Knowledge of God and Love for God originate with these Divine Educators and are the bases for Their teachings. It is this divine aspect of our Love for God that enables each one of us to experience spiritual rebirth and manifest all the 'signs of God'. Without it, lasting inner growth cannot take place.

The fourth type of Love is the Love man shows towards his own kind. It is generally experienced and felt in spontaneous, sudden and unexpected ways that we do not prepare for or control. It can also be experienced in those rare but deliberate acts of self-sacrifice and service to others, whether close to us or not. Little has been divulged to define, describe or otherwise inform us of love given with no expectations or conditions attached. There are obstacles even with acts of altruism which elevate the welfare and happiness of others as a goal without recompense. Unfortunately, most altruistic and humanitarian acts already have a built-in requirement which is seldom acknowledged. They are based upon the condition that the recipient(s) not be emotionally involved with us personally so that we may keep our distance. Altruism is linked more realistically with compassion for those less fortunate than we, but it can be considered a praiseworthy step towards love for the general other.

We must also reluctantly admit that this fourth kind of Love is not romantic love or friendship love. The closest approximation of an unconditioned love is the love of mother for child. Other varieties of human love, while important and even intense, are but fragmented forms of this last kind of Divine

118

Love and upon all of them we have placed certain conditions. So long as these conditions are in effect and met by the recipient, our love prevails. When they are broken or disappear, our love also diminishes or disappears. 'Abdu'l-Bahá spoke about the vagaries of what humans define as true love:

> But the love which sometimes exists between friends is not [true] love, because it is subject to transmutation; this is merely fascination. As the breeze blows, the slender trees yield . . . This kind of love is originated by the accidental conditions of life . . . it is subject to change.
>
> Today you will see two souls apparently in close friendship; tomorrow all this may be changed. Yesterday they were ready to die for one another, today they shun one another's society! This is not love; it is the yielding of the hearts to the accidents of life. When that which has caused this 'love' to exist passes, the love passes also; this is not in reality love.[8]

Like the first type of relative knowledge, conditioned love is the common type of love we all experience. It is also the one which causes us personal problems and gives us the most trouble. The reason for this is that because it is an exclusive type of love its effects are felt in directly obvious and painful ways. It does not occur to us to worry whether or not our love for God or His Love for us will cause us pain. But human love is given selectively along with a set of conditions, and this inevitably hurts others as well as ourselves. What apparently goes wrong is that we confuse giving away our *love* with giving away our *selves*. If this is the case, we will have to learn how we can keep the one and give away the other.

'Abdu'l-Bahá often found Himself in the position of giving advice not only on how genuinely to love others, but on how to get along with those we dislike. His advice proved to be the secret to loving unconditionally. We will also note that He carefully separated *love* from *self*.

The Hows that Love Builds

The Bahá'í secret of loving others is straightforward. It is that one should not draw any distinction between one's love for God, oneself, and one's love for others. When an early Bahá'í believer wanted to know how 'Abdu'l-Bahá could love everyone He met, His reply was that He saw the face of God in everyone. He also

119

admitted that there were those individuals whose personalities made it difficult to love them, but that if we learned to love such people for the sake of God instead of for their personalities, we would learn the secret of true and unconditioned love. 'You will never become angry or impatient if you love them for the sake of God,' He said.[9]

Rather than hypocritically convincing ourselves that we really love those individuals whom we see as having abrasive or negative personalities, we should instead separate the personality from the person, the facade from the inner structure. If we remember that each human being starts life as a 'pure soul' capable of reflecting those virtues we attribute to God, then we can learn to love people for their intrinsic nature and the potentialities of that nature. This is the key to authentic love.

> Individual love cannot be forced and you are not called upon to love everybody personally, but if they are in your lives see to it that they are [the] means of your development and that you are [the] means of their development through your universal love for them.[10]

> ... we must love our enemies for God's sake and because He has created them; we must love them and not for their own personality ... We must love the house for its owner's sake.[11]

Too often we have heard that we cannot love others until we have learned to love ourselves. Although this might seem to be good advice, it is not the key either to self-love or to other-love, for it focuses our love and attention on the personal ego. A healthy love of self is based upon the genuine esteem of self. From this positive self-esteem grow self-worth, self-acceptance and self-confidence. These affective qualities mature not from egoistic love of self but from the knowledge of our core-self.

True identification of self comes about when we identify that innermost core as the human spirit. Otherwise, what we identify is the changeling inside us that is continually seeking a permanent home. There is just no logical way we can ignore or exclude our love for God as the basis which must precede any lasting love we give to ourselves or to others. Once we acknowledge this as the source of all human love, all other kinds of love are rendered more easily. We also receive a bonus; at those times when we seem to have 'run out' of love, we can tap into the infinite source for replenishment.

The Divine Balance

Psychologically, it is counter-productive to demand anything from others, particularly love. Our love should be given as freely as God's Love, which, like the rain, showers all equally. One of our greatest spiritual tests is not only to believe in God's unconditioned Love for us, but to rely utterly upon it. But Bahá'u'lláh says that God's Love cannot reach us unless we first open our hearts to Him. The following explanation by 'Abdu'l-Bahá puts all of these ideals into their highest spiritual perspective:

> The highest love is independent of any personal advantages which we may draw from the love of the friend. If you love truly, your love for your friend will continue, even if he treats you ill. A man who really loves God will love Him whether he be ill, or sad, or unfortunate. He does not love God because He has created him – his life may be full of disassociations and miseries. He does not love God because He has given him health or wealth, because these may disappear at any moment. He does not love Him because He has given him the strength of youth, because old age will surely come upon him. The reason for his love is not because he is grateful for certain mercies and benefits. No!
>
> The lover of God desires and adores Him because He is perfection and because of His perfections. Love should be the very essence of love, and not dependent on outward manifestations.
>
> A moth loves the light, though his wings are burnt. Though his wings are singed, he throws himself against the flame. He does not love the light because it conferred some benefit upon him. Therefore he hovers round the light, though he sacrifices his wings.
>
> This is the highest degree of love. Without this abandonment, this ecstasy, love is imperfect.
>
> The lover of God loves Him for Himself, not for his own sake.[12]

These are not easy words to assimilate into our daily lives for they go against all our popular conventions of what we think love is. Who has truly experienced love on this level? Sometimes, for brief moments, when we see, hear or read about large numbers of people who have gathered together in some unifying

121

cause, we are also able to feel their same intense caring, as though we were one soul in many bodies. Tears often unexpectedly fill our eyes. In the immediacy of this unique moment we experience a oneness with the human race. But we also know that such moments do not last, that the realities of everyday living will intrude to vitiate any permanency. What has happened during those brief moments of experiencing the unification of self with others, is the experiencing of the love of others as the love of God. It is a love that can be sustained if we so desire. It is that reality which should impinge upon 'everyday reality' rather than the reverse, for this reality is certainly the greater reality.

The Valley of Love

In His most mystical work, *The Seven Valleys*, Bahá'u'lláh describes the seven stages through which the soul must pass to reach its final objective, attaining the 'Presence of God'. The first three Valleys are of special concern here. The first is named the Valley of Search, which is what this book is all about, the second is the Valley of Love and the third is the Valley of Knowledge.

It may seem strange that Bahá'u'lláh set the Valley of Knowledge after the Valley of Love, since we have observed that accumulating knowledge is easier than learning how to love. But if we seek the path to God it is necessary first to give up or sacrifice all worldly learning and cultural preconceptions so that we may be bathed with the 'fire of love'. We become as 'little children' awaiting rebirth in the world of Spirit.

Unfortunately, most seekers, after sojourning in the Valley of Search, find it easier to enter the Valley of Knowledge first, assuming that this should be the next step to further spiritual enlightenment. Not only is this not the case, but to continue will lead to the kind of egotistic self-love and self-pride that we have already described, and the seeker will make no further spiritual progress of any kind. After the seeker has found his path to God he must be tested in the crucible of love; only then can he aspire to a knowledge of God.

In the Valley of Love, wrote Bahá'u'lláh, 'is the traveller unaware of himself, and of aught besides himself. He seeth neither ignorance nor knowledge, neither doubt nor certitude; he knoweth not the morn of guidance from the night of error. He fleeth both from unbelief and faith . . .'[13] It is in this Valley that all spiritual transformations begin. 'The steed of this Valley is pain; and if there be no pain this journey will never end.'[14]

As we peel away the glosses of our personality we begin to divest ourselves of those accumulated images and defences that do not succumb easily. Bahá'u'lláh's warning is to 'Free thyself from the fetters of this world, and loose thy soul from the prison of self. Seize thy chance, for it will come to thee no more.'[15]

Bahá'u'lláh speaks to us in the language of the soul. He is not giving us a methodology that we can pre-test and apply using familiar tools. We must listen with our inner ears and understand with our heart of hearts:

> . . . until, like Jacob, thou forsake thine outward eyes, thou shalt never open the eye of thine inward being; and until thou burn with the fire of love, thou shalt never commune with the Lover of Longing . . . Wherefore, O friend, give up thy self that thou mayest find the Peerless One, pass by this mortal earth that thou mayest seek a home in the nest of heaven . . . Wherefore must the veils of the satanic self be burned away at the fire of love, that the spirit may be purified and cleansed . . .[16]

What stands in the way of our attaining the precincts of God are those worldly trappings that reinforce our superficial desires that we have justified as 'needs'. Once we have been baptized by the fire of Love in this Valley, we discover that some of what we have accumulated in life is acceptable and worthy of keeping us company on the remainder of our journey. But, of course, only by completing our journey in the Valley of Knowledge will we know what things we should keep and what things are better left by the wayside.

This mystical path to God is not for everyone, for it requires strict obedience and discipline, a purity of heart and the ability to accept truth no matter what the cost. Identifying and then stripping away our self-delusions and self-deceptions is the most agonizing inner process we will ever have to experience, but it can be borne if God's Love and ours act as a two-way channel. The price of admission into reality is the cost of our illusions and our defences; only then can our inborn desire to love unconditionally surface once more.

Those wayfarers who jump immediately from the Valley of

Search into the Valley of Knowledge may unknowingly remain there for the rest of their lives, intellectually erudite but spiritually dead. There are others who enter the Valley of Love carrying with them such strong attachments to this world and to themselves that these burdens will prevent them from ever leaving. Of all the Valleys, it is the most painful and the most tortuous. Very few travellers escape to the Valley of Knowledge and fewer still travel on to transcend the remaining valleys to reach full spiritual enlightenment.

From the Diary of Juliet

In the early days of the Bahá'í Faith there was an individual who entered the Valley of Love personally guided by 'Abdu'l-Bahá and others close to Him. She recorded this intense experience in a personal diary that recounted how, in almost one instant, all her pretences were stripped away and what was left was the pure human vessel which, for the first time, experienced Divine Love. She was Juliet Thompson, a young, lovely, rich and talented woman who made her home in both Washington DC and New York in the earlier part of this century. She was an artist of note and was listed in the New York Social Register. After the freeing of political and religious prisoners in 1908 by the Young Turks' Rebellion, it was possible for her to make her pilgrimage to the Holy Land to see in person the Master, 'Abdu'l-Bahá, and write of her experience.

Her account is a very personal, intimate and emotional one, since the most direct path for our soul is through our heart, the figurative seat of our emotions. Juliet Thompson, with the kind of direct spiritual help no longer available to any of us, was able to cleanse and sanctify her heart in a comparatively short period of time. This chapter closes with some descriptions of Juliet's feelings and thoughts (which had become intertwined) about her meetings with 'Abdu'l-Bahá and close members of His family and household. The author of the Preface to this recently-published diary writes of Juliet:

> She says here that one early morning . . . she gave up her will, made over her desires and her life to the Will of God, and saw how, when we are able to do that, 'the design takes perfect shape'. Then peace comes, she says, and 'beauty undreamed of blossoms upon our days'.

124

Again she tells how the Master once gathered the American pilgrims together . . . and said He hoped that a great and ever-growing love would be established among them. He knew that their one main desire was to live in His presence, and He told them how this could be done.

'The more', He said, 'you love one another, the nearer you are to me. I go away from this world, but Love stays always.'[17]

For Juliet, who was neither an ordinary nor yet an extra-ordinary person, her awareness was raised to heights few individuals in human history have been privileged to experience. For Juliet, her entire being had become her heart.

Written at the beginning of her pilgrimage in Haifa: I now know what the Master means by the Holy Fragrances. I have come to the centre of their emanation. The air is laden with the Divine Incense – verily, the Breath of God. It is almost unbearable. I am immersed, lost in it. My prayers used to grope through space. Now I am conscious of a close communion with a heart-consuming Spirit of Love, a Spirit more intensely real than the earth and all the stars put together, than the essence of human love, even than mother-love.[18]

Written at her first meeting with several members of the Holy family, in response to an elderly woman who said to her, 'Love is the basis of life': Her intense emotion as she spoke penetrated into the core of our beings. We wept. I rose, bent over her and kissed her and she clasped me in her arms and held me close. Then something within me opened. A fire of love never before experienced in my superficial existence was kindled in my heart from that flame, her heart. By the light of these saints, these torches of God, I see how, even in my deepest moments, my life has been but a shallow stream.[19]

Upon first meeting 'Abdu'l-Bahá, the son Bahá'u'lláh had appointed as His emissary after His ascension, Juliet writes that she was 'struck dumb' and could not speak or move. In her diary she capitalizes all nouns and pronouns that refer to Him. She describes those moments in these words:

The great overwhelming *Spirit* in Him, the divinity of His *Being* deprives one of all one's powers, even the power of sensation, for a time. Yet He makes Himself so simple: in the mercy of His Love, in His great God-tenderness, bends so close to us.[20]

Later she recorded some of the words 'Abdu'l-Bahá spoke to them about divine love.

All the people of the world are patients, are ill. They are in great need of doctors ... [that] they may be cured of their spiritual diseases.

The life of man will at last end in this world. We must all take out of this life some fruit. The tree of one's existence must bear fruit ... And what is the fruit of the human tree? It is the Love of God. It is love for humankind. It is to wish good for all the people of the earth. It is service to humanity. It is truthfulness and honesty. It is virtues and good morals. It is devotion to God. It is the education of souls. Such are the fruits of the human tree. Otherwise it is only wood, nothing else.[21]

She then records 'Abdu'l-Bahá speaking about how difficult attaining the Kingdom of God was:

And should there be no trials, nothing will be accomplished. But when trials appear many will greatly develop. That is to say: those who are sincere believers, firm in the Cause, will develop and advance; but, on the contrary, those who are weak in their faith will *escape*.[22]

And, finally, this entry which describes the moment when Juliet not only feels, but at last understands what is the unconditioned Divine Love of God. 'Abdu'l-Bahá has just asked her if she loves one of the women pilgrims with her:

'Oh yes, my Lord!'
'Very much?'
'Oh so much!' The love already in my heart for Edna was fanned to an intense flame. It burned; it *hurt* me.
'*Very, very* much?'
The Master was still gazing at me, and now I could scarcely *bear* that flame in me, in which my heart itself seemed to be melting away. Tears rained down my cheeks.
'Edna,' cried the Master, 'behold your friend! It is possible for fathers and mothers to weep when their children are in trouble, but it is rare that they weep merely for love of their children, as Juliet has wept for love of you.'
Oh, Heavenly Artist! For one brief moment He had created in me the Love of God; He had given me a foretaste of that Love – other-dimensional, superhuman – which with my whole soul I pray I may attain some day. For without this universal love

how can we hope to work for the Kingdom of God, the oneness of man on earth?

And, in that mysterious moment, I understood that the universal love is not 'impersonal'. I loved not only Edna's soul, but *all* of her. I could have died for her.[23]

9

If Life Follows Death, Where is Time?

Mortal charm shall fade away, roses shall give way to thorns, and beauty and youth shall live their day and be no more. But that which eternally endureth is the Beauty of the True One, for its splendour perisheth not and its glory lasteth for ever; its charm is all-powerful and its attraction infinite.[1]

When the human soul soareth out of this transient heap of dust and riseth into the world of God, then veils will fall away, and verities will come to light, and all things unknown before will be made clear, and hidden truths be understood.

Consider how a being, in the world of the womb, was deaf of ear and blind of eye, and mute of tongue; how he was bereft of any perceptions at all. But once, out of that world of darkness, he passed into this world of light, then his eye saw, his ear heard, his tongue spoke. In the same way, once he hath hastened away from this mortal place into the Kingdom of God, then he will be born in the spirit; then the eye of his perception will open, the ear of his soul will hearken, and all the truths of which he was ignorant before will be made plain and clear.[2]

The Folklore of Death

It is our perceived patterns of reality that define our world, as the Bahá'í teachings repeatedly state. We further condition these perceptions by our subjective preconceptions of how we think we should perceive our reality. These unconscious preconceptions are often more real to us than the percepts upon which

128

they are based. Although these often prejudicial constructs seem to be necessary to make sense of 'the world out there', they have aided our predisposition to concoct fanciful myths regarding 'the world beyond', or life after death.

Cultural anthropologists who study the folklore of both primitive and advanced societies have discovered that life-after-death stories contain similar material. The character and plot devices differ, but the essential story is the same: the dead are punished for their sins by descending into a grotesque netherworld existing inside our planet and the good are carried aloft into a pleasant other-worldly realm. Occasionally paradise exists vaguely somewhere in the mists or 'isles of the West', the geography most generally unexplored by early cultures. We might conclude, therefore, that since so many of these stories agree, our ancestors knew something that we do not. Or it may be more likely that our forebears were bound by up-down, right-left spatial referents that dictated a kind of linear continuity for life after death. In their own way, ideas of reincarnation also restrict themselves to primitive earthly space/time/matter referents, but ones that are cyclical rather than linear.

Bahá'u'lláh rids our imaginations of all such notions and gives us a deeply profound way of looking at death and existence beyond this life. These ideas are quite different from anything we have grown up with or presently hold.

The Myth of Annihilation

Any explanation of the continuation of life after this life must resolve what we might call the spiritual 'three body problem': how will the effects of energy- and space/time-bound matter be reconciled with the continuation of the individuality of the human spirit in an afterlife?

Is it even correct to say that 'death' occurs at all? What happens to our individual consciousness – does it continue unchanged? Can death be viewed as only another form of change or transmutation?

We already know that all energy in the universe transforms itself for re-use. Death, as a physical event, may be more appropriately referred to as the cessation of those biological functions required to maintain the conditions necessary for this organic life. If this is the case, then we can infer that our unique

THE BAHÁ'Í TEACHINGS

human energy, the human spirit, may become available for re-
use and transformation on another level. But where and how
could this transformation occur?

We have already pointed out that high-energy physicists
observe an almost unintelligible level of existence in the sub-
atomic world where the usual notions of space and time and
matter do not apply and where strange dimensional transactions
take place. In that world, space/time/matter become what the
physicist says they are. Relativity still applies, but it seems to
obey a different rule, that of probability.

For example, the negative charge of an atom, the electron, can
be defined as either energy or mass, as can the free atom itself,
thus defying a proper definition of matter. As for the space the
electron occupies, it does and it doesn't; it may occupy all its
space simultaneously, or perhaps only a part, since no instru-
ment has actually isolated an electron to know for certain. Even
time, to utilize a pun, is immaterial to the electron. To its
counterpart, the proton, or positive charge of energy, time is also
meaningless, since it apparently will never decay and will exist
for the duration of the universe. If it were possible for the most
simple atom to communicate with us to give us its point of view
of the universe as the atom experienced it, the picture conveyed
would be beyond our wildest imaginings.

Using another analogy, imagine that a mother-to-be and her
embryo were given the power to communicate with each other.
The mother would describe her world using space/time/matter
referents totally incomprehensible to her unborn. How would
she tell of colours, of music, of the sciences, language, the
beauties of nature and even the pleasure of eating food to a life-
form that had not yet developed the powers of reason or the
sensibilities of seeing, hearing, tasting, smelling and so on.

In a way, communication of sorts does take place between
representatives of this world and the embryonic world, perhaps
more accurately described as 'influences' rather than language
communication. Who can deny that the unborn child is influenced
by what the mother and her obstetrician do?

Comparing the world to come to this life and the life of the
embryo is a recurring analogy in the Bahá'í Writings. 'The
world beyond is as different from this world as this world is
different from that of the child while still in the womb of its
mother.'[3] 'Abdu'l-Bahá also used this analogy in a talk He gave

in Washington, DC in referring to the *Titanic* disaster. He observed that the embryo is reluctant to be born into a strange new world where its own kind of material comforts will be no more. But once having arrived, were it capable of making immediate comparisons, the superiority of this world would be so obvious that, given a choice, it would not agree to go back to its previous immobilized life. Yet many people base their belief in an afterlife contingent upon the 'coming back' or communication of someone who has died. Who among us would choose to 'go back' to the world inside the womb?

Bahá'u'lláh and 'Abdu'l-Bahá also compare the life to follow to the experiences of our dream-world. They tell us it is the closest approximation to describing how a different space/time/matter existence can be just as real to us as the one we experience in our waking hours. In our dreams, They point out, we are physically, mentally and emotionally participating in a reality that during its elapsed time is the *only* reality. Yet these experiences are enacted somewhere within another portion of our brains to which our conscious minds have relinquished control. Is it possible that consciousness might exist on more than one level? This question has a number of profound implications that are only beginning to be addressed. So far, no one has completely solved the mechanics of dreams as it relates to either the consciousness of animals or of humans.

The two examples cited above, the embryo's world and our dream-world, suggest that the promise of another kind of existence should cause us neither fear nor reluctance. It is not the actual condition of death we fear, but its expectation, and the possible annihilation of self.

The conception of annihilation is a factor in human degradation, a cause of human debasement and lowliness, a source of human fear and abjection. It has been conducive to the dispersion and weakening of human thought whereas the realization of existence and continuity has upraised man to sublimity of ideals, established the foundations of human progress and stimulated the development of heavenly virtues; therefore it behooves man to abandon thoughts of non-existence and death which are absolutely imaginary and see himself ever living, everlasting in the divine purpose of his creation. He must turn away from ideas which degrade the human soul, so that day by day and hour by hour he may

131

THE BAHÁ'Í TEACHINGS

advance upward and higher to spiritual perception of the
continuity of the human reality. If he dwells upon the thought
of non-existence he will become utterly incompetent; with
weakened will-power his ambition for progress will be lessened
and the acquisition of human virtues will cease.[4]

The Riddle of Time

We can understand more about the life/death process if we
understand that the conservation of energy is a universal law
affecting all things and if we can solve our spiritual three-body
problem. We will propose that if we can solve the riddle of time,
the perplexities of space and matter will also disappear. We
know that time, space and matter are like three interlocking
rings intertwined in such a way that if any one of them is
removed, all are immediately disconnected. Their manifested
realities are determined by the one reality of the Divine Spirit/
Energy. This would indicate that our two riddles are, in fact,
only one riddle. It reduces our spiritual three-body problem to a
'unified-body' problem. We will use the term 'dimensional time'
to mean space/time/matter.

We should now be able to talk about the various permutations
of this universal Energy in a religious context without the need
to resort to the sciences. So far, the two common examples
already given, the world of the embryo and the world of dreams,
hint at other states of consciousness that are provable both
subjectively and objectively. Might not there exist additional
states, as yet unknown to us?

These words of 'Abdu'l-Bahá, quoted in a previous chapter,
will be our touchstone for further explorations: 'There are two
kinds of eternities. There is an eternity of essence, that which is
without first cause, and an eternity of time, that which has no
beginning.'[5] The following arguments and explanations derive
from the above statements.

Mortality and Immortality

Our first permutation of dimensional time will be to reconsider
the idea of mortality and immortality. We wrongly assume that
immortality and eternality are synonymous. The word 'eternal-

ity' is coined to described the foreverness of the absolute state, while the word 'eternity' denotes the state itself.

Both mortality and immortality are time-bound concepts, that is, concepts that belong to our familiar world of conditioned relativities. They imply two conditions or states rather than the one absolute condition or state implied by the idea of eternity. 'Abdu'l-Bahá observed, 'Therefore, the idea of mortality presupposes the existence of immortality – for if there were no Life Eternal, there would be no way of measuring the life of this world!'[6] Measurements always take place in dimensional time.

Mortality refers to created organisms that have received life at some particular point in time and are subject to decomposition or death at another point in time. There is a 'when' and another 'when' to connect these two events together on a linear scale.

Immortality gives us only one 'when' – that moment when a created organism comes into visible existence. It is a linear continuum which has a beginning, but no ending in time. The idea of immortality denies annihilation for created life. Annihilation means non-being and non-existence. 'Abdu'l-Bahá clarifies the difference between death and non-existence in a universe where complete annihilation is impossible:

Non-existence therefore is an expression applied to change of form, but this transformation can never be rightly considered annihilation, for the elements of composition are ever present and existent as we have seen in the journey of the atom through successive kingdoms, unimpaired; hence there is no death; life is everlasting ... death is only a relative term implying change ... Through his ignorance, man fears death; but the death he shrinks from is imaginary and absolutely unreal; it is only human imagination ... For existence there is neither change nor transformation; existence is ever existence; it can never be translated into non-existence. It is gradation; a degree below a higher degree is considered as non-existence. This dust beneath our feet, as compared with our being, is non-existent. When the body crumbles into dust we can say it has become non-existent; therefore its dust in relation to living forms of human being is as non-existent but in its own sphere it is existent, it has its mineral being. Therefore it is well proved that absolute non-existence is impossible; it is only relative ... [God] has endowed the phenomenal world with being, it is impossible for that world to become non-being, for it

133

is the very genesis of God; it is in the realm of origination; it is a creational and not a subjective world, and the bounty descending upon it is continuous and permanent.[7]

If the created world existed only as our subjective experiencing of it, as some believe, then it would logically follow that being, once losing its subjective state, would also cease to exist. This would mean that existence, or creation, was dependent upon each individual's realization and confirmation of it, and when this subjective awareness ceased, that portion of existence would also cease. 'Abdu'l-Bahá argues that individual consciousness is not a determinant of creation either as a whole or as a part; nor does any individual's birth or death increase or decrease existence as a whole, or as a part. The individuation of the Divine Spirit/Energy does not 'cause' a part of creation either to increase or decrease by its manifestations in any of the kingdoms of existence.

'Abdu'l-Bahá's explanation also points out that whatever is mortal partakes of immortality in a very special way. Once created, the basic atoms of life remain unchanged and untransformed. What does change are the complex molecular compositions that atoms form; it is these compositions which have a transient life and are therefore mortal. Looked at another way, everything created in our universe is immortal on one level or another, since all matter reverts back to its fundamental elemental nature.

But what, you ask, of me? Being creatures who are subjectively conscious of our own individualities, we want to know about our own special form of immortality. But at this point, the question is still premature. The answer to this question will continue to elude us until we unravel even more of the puzzling nature of time. For if life follows death, where and what is our human spirit/energy?

The illustration below will help us find our way to the solution. Our clues derive from a reference by Bahá'u'lláh in *The Seven Valleys*:

On this same basis, ponder likewise the differences among the worlds. Although the divine worlds be never ending, yet some refer to them as four: The world of time, which is the one that hath both a beginning and an end; the world of duration, which hath a beginning, but whose end is not revealed; the world of perpetuity, whose beginning is not to be seen but which is known to have an end; and the world of eternity, neither a beginning nor an end of which is visible.[8]

Immediately following this description, Bahá'u'lláh recounts the four pathways of Divine Love, His key for unravelling the above passage. We will enter those four worlds He called time, duration, perpetuity and eternity to see if they will resolve more of the mysteries of life after death.

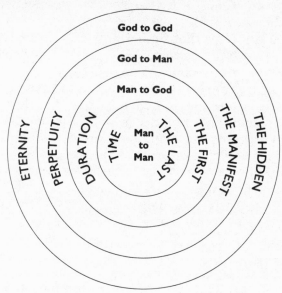

The World of Time

The world of relative time refers to our subjective experiencing of it. We measure time as if it were a straight line dividing the past, the present and the future. Because of its many conditions, it is the least predictable and the most mercurial of the four aspects of time mentioned by Bahá'u'lláh. Just as the Circadians experience time in their own subjective way, we experience ours in our own way. Even the 'same' time can appear to slow down or to accelerate, depending upon who is doing the experiencing of its 'passage'. As we grow older and more sedentary, we notice that time seems to accelerate as our lives move more slowly. Conversely, the more quickly we experience the passage of time, the more it seems to slow down. Science tells us that if we could move faster than the speed of light, relative time would cease to exist! The rate at which light waves travel is the closest approximation to an objective or universal standard time that we currently know.

Variations in the rate of time also hold true for our inner world of dreams. There is as yet no plausible explanation how the passage of time is controlled in our dreams. In sleep, time passes at an accelerated rate, so that events that might take hours to complete in wake-time are completed in minutes in dream-time. Both 'times' are real because our subjective experiences of them are real.

How certain can we be that time would exist if the participant were not conscious of its passage? (We are all participants, not observers, in our dimensional time world.) For example, as embryos we had no awareness or memory of the passage of time, so how can we be certain it had any reality? Time may be nothing more than an atomic clock. If the neutrino could consciously measure its life-span, for example, would it think it had 'lived' a long time? There seems to be not one solution but a variety of solutions to the riddle of relative time and how it affects the differing levels of consciousness in all the kingdoms of existence. Apparently, it all depends upon *who* is measuring it and *how*. Time seems to be our invention after all.

The World of Duration

In the world of duration, time has a beginning but no visible ending; therefore all things existing in this world must also have a beginning but no discernible end. This also decribes the state of immortality.

This world is founded upon the relationship of created things – which have both beginnings and endings – to the Absolute, which has neither. Since all creation is a manifestation of Spirit, all things partake of immortality in some form of continued fundamental existence, as we have already discussed. But it is only the human soul which continues its existence on a non-fundamental level and continues its evolution into other worlds and realms as energy/spirit. Since the human spirit can never merge to become one with God, its journey never ends. Its spiritual evolution is *'the approaching unto God* ... The soul does not evolve from degree to degree as a law – it only evolves nearer to God, by the Mercy and Bounty of God.'[9]

In this world of duration also exist those eternal signs and attributes of God that He has bestowed upon man in their fullness and upon all creation in lesser degrees. For example, only in the human kingdom can love, perfection and knowledge seek their ultimate realizations as Divine Love, Divine Perfections and Divine Knowledge. As divine ideals, their acquisitions do not end in time but in the infinite world of God.

Perhaps the timelessness experienced by the non-decaying proton also takes place in this world of duration. It is possible that the secrets of these three worlds of time may be locked and hidden in the first and most ubiquitous example of all created matter, the primordial hydrogen atom. If this can be true of the atom, then our own selves – the summation of all atomic creation – must contain those answers in an even more abundant and comprehensive form.

The World of Perpetuity

In this world there is an ending but no beginning, for what exists here originates with God in His Divine Unity. Here reside all potentialities that God may or may not will into creation. All possibilities emerge from this realm to find their purpose, their goal and their end. When given form and meaning these potentialities define God's relation to His creation – the eternality (no beginning) of their essence and the mortality (an ending) of their substance. As God's signs and attributes, all the kingdoms of existence become their objectives. Their highest goal and complete repository, however, is the human kingdom. All of humanity's potentialities and possibilities for fulfilling its high station derive from this divine world. The world of perpetuity is the mirror image of the world of duration; both reflect the face of eternity.

Eternity

Eternity is not another definition of dimensional time. Eternity is the absolute standard from which all beginnings and endings flow and return, circle and gather. As objective time, it encompasses all aspects of subjective time. In 'real' Reality, the world of God, only one time exists. Like our description of Reality, Eternity is the Time that encompasses all other times and gives them definition. Our connection with Eternity is the same connection we have with Reality; although we come from that Reality, we ourselves are not that Reality. Eternity is God's time, absolute and single. Only those who have awakened their souls have the capacity to discover this truth and to realize at last that everyone already lives in all four worlds of time simultaneously! The world of past/present/future, of duration and of perpetuity all become the same 'time' that each of us can experience inwardly as well as outwardly. We may eventually escape time, but we can never escape Eternity.

Further Permutations of Time

In the Qur'án Muḥammad alludes to this mystical quaternary of the four worlds of time as representing the full condition of Divinity, saying, 'He is the First and the Last, the Manifest and the Hidden; and He is the Knower of all things.'[10] In Christianity it becomes a direct echo of Judaic mysticism that the apocalyptic writer, John, has the future universal Messiah proclaim as His station in God: 'I am Alpha and Omega, the beginning and the end, the first and the last.'[11]

Bahá'u'lláh makes many references to 'the Hidden and the Manifest', and 'the First and the Last' in His explanations of the Divine Unity and the divine station of the Holy Messengers. He also cites these four worlds as a description of how the spiritual condition of man connects with divinity.

When explaining the station of the Holy Teachers in their relationship to God, Bahá'u'lláh writes: 'They are all the manifestation of the "Beginning" and the "End", the "First" and the "Last", the "Seen" and the "Hidden" – all of which pertain to Him Who is the Innermost Spirit of Spirits and Eternal Essence of Essences.'[12]

He then reveals in what ways these four metaphysical states also refer to man:

Although a brief example hath been given concerning the beginning and ending of the relative world, the world of attributes, yet a second illustration is now added, that the full meaning may be manifest. For instance, let thine Eminence consider his own self; thou art first in relation to thy son, last in relation to thy father. In thine outward appearance, thou tellest of the appearance of power in the realms [of] divine creation; in thine inward being thou revealest the hidden mysteries which are the divine trust deposited within thee. And thus firstness and lastness, outwardness and inwardness are, in the sense referred to, true of thyself, that in these four states conferred upon thee thou shouldst comprehend the four divine states, and that the nightingale of thine heart on all the branches of the rosetree of existence, whether visible or concealed, should cry out: 'He is the first and the last, the Seen and the Hidden . . .'

These statements are made in the sphere of that which is relative, because of the limitations of men.[13]

He ends this passage by suggesting that those few personages who have traversed the worlds of limitations to dwell on the plane of the Absolute have no need of such allusions, because 'in this realm, the first is the last itself, and the last is but the first'.[14]

Speaking of the eternality of the human spirit, 'Abdu'l-Bahá also refers directly to these other aspects of time (italics are the author's). He says:

Nevertheless, the spirit in its original state, in its own spiritual perception, will be *eternal* and *perpetual*; it neither finds any imperfection, nor will it become crippled . . . it neither becomes ill from the diseases of the body nor cured by its health . . . it is evident and certain that the spirit is different from the body, and that its *duration* is independent of that of the body; on the contrary, the spirit with the utmost greatness rules in the world of the body, and its power and influence, like the bounty of the sun in the mirror, are apparent and visible. But when the mirror becomes dusty or breaks, it will cease to reflect the rays of the sun.[15]

The central idea in these spiritual metaphors of time is that they are hints to different invisible states and conditions enclosed within our clock-work time. The model used here describes only four states for simplicity's sake and for their consistency with the four kinds of Divine Love and Knowledge.

This Bahá'í model of time allows us to picture both our physical and our spiritual connection with all creation and with the Divine in a new conceptual framework. In comparison to God the Hidden, the hidden nature of our own spiritual being becomes more real and accessible. In the same way we are able to grasp how our 'lastness' in the order of the creational hierarchy becomes the 'first' to recognize and worship God.

What of Me Remains?

We can now put into place the last piece of the puzzle of life after death: what remains of our subjective consciousness or the awareness of self? Chapter Four made the observation that although the animal possesses consciousness, it is not aware of its consciousness. We argued that animal consciousness is experienced as instincts, basic emotions and rudimentary intelligence, and works for the survival of the animal. As far as the animal is concerned, they operate as one inner condition which controls the animal's behaviour. Many humans assume that what holds true for the animal must hold true for us, that is, consciousness is a push-button inner template that controls all our behaviour, much like artificial or simulated intelligence in state-of-the-art computers. This point of view denies the uniqueness of the individual human psyche and explains consciousness on its most basic level, that of memory functioning through the chemistry of the brain.

The Bahá'í point of view sees the human psyche as a special creation containing all the biological degrees and levels of consciousness and which cannot be explained merely as a more complex function of neurons and synapses. Animal consciousness and human consciousness may share similarities but they are not identical. It is the Divine Spirit/Energy that is the universal unity, not consciousness.

The Bahá'í model allows us to expand this idea further. The theory of the hierarchic nature of reality suggests that each gradient of existence experiences whatever 'consciousness' has already been encoded into that plane. Furthermore, it suggests that within each level itself various degrees of consciousness or self-awareness are possible for its members. That is, animal consciousness cannot transcend into human consciousness but within the animal kingdom, even within the same species, consciousness will be uniquely individualized. We have noticed these 'similar differences' in our pet dogs or cats who have distinct personalities but which are recognizable as distinctly 'cat' or 'dog' personalities. In the case of people, we are all endowed with the human consciousness prescribed by our niche in the natural order of things, but within our niche a vast continuum from deep to light degrees of consciousness can be experienced to enrich our lives. We are so circumscribed by our own experienced awareness of self and others that it is difficult to imagine another or different kind of consciousness.

It is even more difficult to imagine an afterlife without our own familiar individualized consciousness as the centre of our selfhood. In this life it is true that our subjective consciousness gives us our sense of identity and purpose; without it, we would be at a loss to explain how reasoning life could continue, let alone exist. The question that challenges us, then, is what remains of us as individuals upon the cessation of this life if our *self* consciousness also undergoes a transformation?

Much of what we have accumulated in this life has little to do with those qualities and perfections our human spirit will be able to make use of in its next life. We will not, for example, carry with us our acquired social personalities, our sexual passions or our physical skills. Bahá'u'lláh wrote, 'How can any one imagine that man's consciousness and personality will be maintained, when the very instruments necessary to their existence and function will have completely disintegrated?'[16]

What we do retain, He says, is our innate character as it has matured through a lifetime of effort and discipline. We can think of this basic self as our authentic self – whatever we have made of it. As an analogy, Bahá'u'lláh informs us that in the same way the embryo develops in the womb those things it will need for this life – eyes, ears, vocal chords, self-awareness, etc. – so do we unconsciously develop those sensibilities that we will need in our next life. What these sensibilities are precisely, we do not know. If we did know, we would attempt to dissect and analyze them in order to utilize them here and now. If this were possible to do, we would enter the next world spiritually crippled and deformed.

Exact information concerning the soul's state and condition after death will never be fully revealed by any future Holy Revelator, according to Bahá'u'lláh. 'The nature of the soul after death can never be described, nor is it meet and permissible to reveal its whole character to the eyes of men.'[17] This denial comes about not due to the ignorance of the Holy Teachers but to the perversity of humankind who would misuse such knowledge.

141

What Their teachings do reveal concerning this state is that the human spirit, upon leaving this world

> . . . will evince such ascendancy, and reveal such influence as no force on earth can equal.[18]

> [It] will continue to progress until it attaineth the presence of God, in a state and condition which neither the revolution of ages and centuries, nor the changes and chances of this world, can alter. It will endure as long as the Kingdom of God, His sovereignty, His dominion and power will endure.[19]

> Certain fruits, indeed, attain their fullest development only after being severed from the tree.[20]

Just as we cannot imagine a condition of awareness that is not totally subjective, so we cannot imagine an existence exempt from personal interests, desires and fears. Bahá'u'lláh suggests that the purified soul connects with other souls in those worlds, and the powers and joys become so intensified that we will wonder at ever having lived as separate tiny candles, alone with our flickering light, when in the worlds to come we will blaze as one radiant force. We are assured that if we could be given a foretaste of experiencing this world of eternal illumination, we would never desire to go back to this material world. In fact, all our instinctual human desires and fears will disappear to become one pre-phenomenal fear and desire – the awe of God and the yearning to return to Him.

Of course, not every human soul will begin its renewed existence equally. Some individuals have striven for spiritual maturity while others have denied any reality at all to their souls. Some have so degraded their human station that their existence in the next world is comparable to that of the mineral in this world. Still, at the hour of death, the Bahá'í Writings affirm, such an individual may pray to God for his soul's salvation, or another may pray or intercede on his behalf, and, depending upon the mercy and bounty of God, such a soul may attain a place in the next life. We are warned that no one has the right to judge another soul, either while living or at death. 'Abdu'l-Bahá also made it clear that the 'heaven and hell' of existence is not confined to this world but that spiritual rewards and punishments continue in all the worlds of God.

In all the worlds of God nothing remains stationary –

everything either progresses or declines, since motion is God's essential and fundamental law. This law applies as well to the human spirit after death. But its progress, as 'Abdu'l-Bahá pointed out, is commensurate with its state or degree. That is, the human soul can never attain the reality of a Bahá'u'lláh or a Christ. Its continued acquisition of the divine gifts and favours in all the divine realms is conditioned by its original creational level. Its eternal purpose is to draw ever nearer to God and enter the precincts of His presence.

The final answer to 'what remains of me?' will not soothe or appease the human ego which feeds upon its own importance. Individual self-awareness remains, but not in a condition our dimensional-time consciousness would recognize. In addition, a new awareness is added – that of participating in and sharing the awareness of others as our own.

Preparation for this expansion of self begins in this life whenever we experience that special bonding with others that we called 'unconditioned love' in the previous chapter. Remembering those special moments, we admit that instead of the 'loss of self' there has been an *addition* to self. If all of us were able to telepathize both our thoughts and feelings to each other we would experience this kind of empathetic joining of consciousnesses, as the Circadians in our fable were finally learning to master. We, too, would learn at last what the Revelators of God mean by becoming 'one soul in many bodies'. Once experienced, we would wonder at our callousness in this life. One of the lessons to be learned in this life is that we are not alone and that our welfare is inseparable from and dependent upon the welfare of other single lives.

This special 'coming together' of divine perfections such as love and knowledge in the next level of existence opens our self-referential type of consciousness to other realms of consciousness in worlds of God undreamed of in our familiar earth-bound experiences. What were once fragmented human spirits in this world are gathered together and made whole in the next. There they are drawn towards the Centre of Reality, the home of the Eternal. Metaphorically speaking, it is the home our hearts never left.

10

Resurgence, Convergence and Synthesis

Every imperfect soul is self-centred and thinketh only of his own good. But as his thoughts expand a little he will begin to think of the welfare and comfort of his family. If his ideas still more widen, his concern will be the felicity of his fellow citizens; and if still they widen, he will be thinking of the glory of his land and of his race. But when ideas and views reach the utmost degree of expansion and attain the stage of perfection, then will he be interested in the exaltation of humankind. He will then be the well-wisher of all men and the seeker of the weal and prosperity of all lands. This is indicative of perfection.

Thus, the divine Manifestations of God had a universal and all-inclusive conception. They endeavoured for the sake of everyone's life and engaged in the service of universal education.[1]

Every universal cause is divine and every particular one is temporal.[2]

Love ye all the religions and all races with a love that is true and sincere and show that love through deeds and not through the tongue; for . . . the majority of men are, in speech, well-wishers, while action is best.[3]

Models and General Systems

The spiritual model of the universe that this book has presented does not presume to be an exact replica of Reality on any level. Models can only suggest and hint at the laws that govern creation; they do better at picturing a portion of the reality that theories attempt to reconstruct. Truth, on any human level, is never exact.

This book has not attempted to pit one 'proof' against another; only by using the grammar of logic or mathematical equations can anyone 'prove' that A equals B. But as any good scientist or philosopher knows, the truths about Reality are only approximated. How accurate they are can be determined only by how well they survive the tests of falsification. To make statements no one can either refute or prove about the nature of things, e.g., 'the world will end next year', is to be intellectually irresponsible. For a scientist to demand, 'Prove that God exists!' is just as irresponsible as the religionist's answer, 'Prove that He doesn't!' 'Proof' is neither the solution nor the issue. In the case for or against God, the issue is whether or not we have a universe that works more efficiently with an intelligent originating principle, and whether or not such a proposition can illuminate or explain other phenomena.

A good theoretical model should also call attention to heretofore hidden and possibly unexplainable aspects of our reality worlds. And, like any work of art, a model should be aesthetically pleasing and tantalize the observer so that he wants to come back to it again and again. What can it explain? How can it be applied? What are its flaws? How reliable is it? In short, what will it do?

These kinds of choices for 'doing' are usual in both scientific and philosophic endeavours but are not generally associated with religious choices. The intellectual tends to see religion as primarily an emotional response, an acceptance of non-reasoned faith. For a Bahá'í, true faith is an expression combining both will and love, not a leap of intuition. Using this criterion, a workable model of faith should lead to action based upon this kind of unshakable certitude and not upon blind acceptance.

One of the most inclusive and understandable models for picturing our physical and our social universes is that offered by General System Theory (GST) developed by Ludwig von Bertalanffy in the 1920s. Currently, it is the only theoretical model whose parameters can be easily superimposed upon the Bahá'í model. Its methodology can also be applied to study religions as living social systems.

A general or open system, as opposed to a mechanical or closed

145

system, is made up of one or more individual components whose intra-relationships create a network of interactions which evolve into a unique and synergistic 'whole'. As an organic entity it also creates its own environment and boundaries which help to identify it. Maintaining itself takes a constant influx of energy; the input of energy is obtained from the outside and recycled inside to provide its nourishment. The more simple organic systems need for their growth and stimulation provisions such as air, sunlight, food and water. As the complexities of living systems increase, their requirements begin to include non-biological intangibles such as information and nurturing. In human beings these intangibles explode into a vast array and variety of needs and wants, elements both desirable and undesirable, healthy and unhealthy, and an almost constant bombardment of vague and undefined stimuli we unconsciously attempt to sort out.

Whatever is taken in by a self-organizing system is processed internally by what some system-generalists call 'negative feedback' which allows the system to recycle its input in a proper mix that will maintain the balance and stability it needs to persist over time and produce a perceptible result such as an action or work of some kind. 'Positive feedback', another term borrowed from engineering, occurs when foreign or unusual elements enter the system and disrupt its equilibrium. In a socio-cultural system such an intrusion may become so significant that its effects create a magnification process that can result in irreversible change or transformation of the entire system, producing either a constructive result, such as a renaissance, or a destructive result, a dictatorship, for example.

Everything in our universe can be called a system in its own right as well as a sub-system of a larger system, or a larger system containing smaller, lesser systems, each hierarchically organized. From ecosystems to family systems, from planetary systems to individual biological systems – all can be envisaged in this way.

Evolving living systems are distinguished in other ways. To remain open, a system must allow for the infusion of new and vibrant energy which is vital to its continued efficiency and health. It is also becoming more apparent that successful open systems begin with or acquire a 'reason for existence', a purpose, which seems necessary for its sub-systems to adopt and support.

In human social systems this centre or core is usually a person, an ideology, a cause or all three.

Because all organic systems evolve by natural law, which is the same as divine law, they seek the ultimate goal of completion or closure. Translated into spiritual language this means that all natural systems seek perfection. But because the individual components making up any system are not created in a perfected condition, total closure or completion can never take place. Perfection, as we have noted before, describes potentiality. When a social or religious system attempts closure by presuming its own perfection, it has, in fact, issued its own death warrant. Perfection for any human system is open-ended, the 'carrot-on-the-stick' which not only motivates and inspires the system but is its goal and its purpose. Divine religions are the first to point this out, and as imperfect individuals we sense this lure of perfectibility and are drawn to those great spiritual organizations.

Currently, more and more scholars are discovering that the general systems framework provides the ideal commonality which the various disciplines have long been seeking to unify their reality bases. Many scientists and engineers from the applied sciences have incorporated the salient features of General System Theory and methodology to help categorize and explain large or conflicting pieces of data. Social scientists, psychologists, educators and ecologists have been applying both its theory and its methods successfully for many years. To study anything that grows and evolves, its framework is ideal.

Religions as General Systems

GST can easily be applied to study those evolutionary systems we call the world's great religions. Each began as a small group of people brought together by a shared belief in its Founder's infallibility. He is its centre and its core around which everything else revolves. In its formative period the religion's energy is derived from the vitality of the Prophet and His teachings which draw people to it like a magnet and becomes its *raison d'être*. The infant system organizes itself around this core with the help of charismatic leaders and teachers. Soon the pure and unadulterated energy of its teachings is replaced by a

147

carefully controlled input of outside influences to protect the newly-gained prestige and power of its centralized authority to 'interpret' the Founder's message. As the years roll by, the system becomes so entrenched in fabricated rituals and dogma that it begins to resemble a closed or mechanical system. Its end-product is no longer spiritual wisdom and self-transformation but an official canon that its followers must accept as 'truth'. The original message and teachings of its Founder are reshaped to suit each new cultural mind-set. Over an even longer period of time, its artificially-created boundaries become so fixed and rigid that they prevent new information or energy from entering that would allow for adaptation and change. As a result, its internal organizational processes become so repetitious and stratified that its leaders must use the psychological tools of indoctrination, intimidation and guilt to retain both its power and its adherents.

Populations of static or closed systems can be more easily controlled than those inhabiting open-ended ones. History has also furnished evidence that such isolative systems can endure almost indefinitely so long as their input/output processes are strictly and centrally controlled. Unfortunately, this also means that by maintaining such a precarious equilibrium between the energy/information from the outside wanting to get in with the natural process of entropy already taking place within, in time the system's internal feedback mechanisms will no longer be adaptive enough to prevent the eventual break-down of the total system. Following the natural course of events, entropy wins. It is at this point that God renews His bond with mankind and provides the powerful catalyst needed to renew and transform the existing system in the form of a new revelation. The older religion not only resists this insurgence of fresh energy, but actively seeks to destroy the intruder which will change the *status quo*.

All successful social movements also appear to have followed this sequence of events, with minor variations, in the course of their development. It is not certain whether all social systems *must* follow this basic pattern in order to survive; and in the case of religions, the progress of the Bahá'í Faith should be followed closely. As the world's newest revelation, its administrative organization has built into it changes for both its elected leadership on all levels and many of its internal procedures, allowing for growth and evolution within each sub-system, as well as in the overall system.

Resurgence

The primary source of outside energy for a divine religion is God Himself, transmitted through the agency of the Holy Spirit. As a source, it is inexhaustible. From age to age there is a sudden and overpowering resurgence of this energy when a new Revelator is chosen to regenerate the existing inflexible religious system which is no longer capable or willing to effect its own transformation. No Revelator from God ever planned the demise of any existing religion; in fact, He repeatedly praises His predecessor and His teachings. The new Teacher's intent is to revitalize and revivify an ailing society with new social principles and laws and increase the spiritual knowledge, health and guidance of its individuals. Nor has any Holy Prophet tried to deceive His followers or to use His revelatory powers to His own advantage. He acts with the knowledge that the social balance will be upset, that there will be a shift of religious authority, and that a certain amount of disorder and disequilibrium (positive feedback) will result as the new, unfamiliar and untried system supersedes the old.

Each successive revelation moves outward and beyond the boundaries of the previous one like the surging waves of an expanding ocean. The gift of revelation becomes the resurgence of human genius as well.

Unfortunately, this kind of transfer of religious energy/information has never taken place on our planet. What should have been one continuing peaceful progression of revelation became instead separated and isolated religious organizations, each suspicious of and hostile to the other. The outcome of this universal anomaly has been both destructive and oppressive to humanity whose societies provide out-dated, ready-made, but differing religious doctrines that assume unquestioned acceptance and loyalty. It is true that the world today does not need *another* religion; what it needs is for the existing divine religions to acknowledge their common single origin and embark upon a programme of universal spiritual re-education.

We can only wonder at what kind of world we would now inhabit if all the major religions had in fact become one continuing and progressive religion, analogous to the development of Western science. If we could at this very moment grasp the implications of this astonishing possibility for the growth and maturity of the human race, it would be like seeing the future from this glimpse of today. We would very likely see the world as one human family united spiritually, racially and politically, with people having at last outgrown their strange desire for war.

For the Bahá'í this vision of the future means a new system, a new order and a new earth. This ideal is not just another utopian fantasy, another claim to be able to establish the 'perfect society'. Such a claim could be realized only if every individual on earth attained perfection. Chapter Seven argued that what is realistically possible to achieve is the perfecting *process* – a process our engineering technologies apply every day, whether they are producing better toasters, computers or spacecraft. This little by little, better by better progressive striving for the 'best' is possible of achievement not only by our sciences, but by our governments, by our social orders and by our religions.

We forget that even the divinely-revealed religions belong to the world of relativities and so can be studied objectively. Each has been conditioned by the time in history in which it has arisen and by the culture and religion into which its Prophet has been born. Eventually, as is the fate of any open system existing in historic time, every religion must also live out its appointed life of birth, fruition, maturity, and finally death, and make way for the new cycle.

Over a hundred years ago Bahá'u'lláh pronounced that 'the world's equilibrium hath been upset through the vibrating influence of this most great, this new World Order. Mankind's ordered life hath been revolutionized through the agency of this unique, this wondrous System – the like of which mortal eyes have never witnessed.'4

For over a hundred years the older religious, social, economic and political systems have been in transition, having moved from mediaevalism, or controlled progress in isolation, to the new age of transnationalism, where the progress and productivity of one nation accrues to all nations. The catalyst for this universal renaissance may indeed be the Bahá'í Faith, that 'wondrous System' capable of revivifying and transforming all the niches of civilization.

Convergence

In a sceptical age that has separated religious truth from scientific and philosophical truth, we are nonetheless beginning to see the unmistakable signs of a confluence in certain areas of scientific and religious thought. The new discoveries in particle physics agree basically with the picture of the universe and man that the mystical elements of the world's religions describe. Science is now finding evidence that the same universal truths exist in the heart of the atom that exist in the heart of God. Only the terminology differs.

Both the disciplines of the social sciences and philosophy continue to resist this framework for examining an interrelated universe in which all things interact and influence each other. While some social scientists are currently seeing the need for reassessment, philosophy has come to the proverbial fork in the road but vacillates as to which path it should take. It continues to restrict its questions to an either/or universe which results in irreconcilable answers. The message of contemporary philosophy seems to be that existence is a subjective experiencing of historic time that is given reality only by how we choose to interpret it. There is no essence, no thing-in-itself, no intrinsic meaning to life. We are the 'something' that grew out of 'nothing'.

The three current dominating schools of thought – existentialism, language or linguistic philosophy and behavioural philosophy – wrestle primarily with the question of what constitutes objective and/or subjective reality. As we shall see in the following brief descriptions of their main features, what they all have in common is a restrictive egocentricity, that is, in each one the collective individual is the standard for measuring all things.

Existentialism

Existentialism continues to be the most popular of these three because it consists of a large but vague middle and an excluded beginning and ending which allows its spokespersons great latitude in describing its contents. Because it has no systematic structure, the explanations and interpretations of its adherents are sometimes contradictory. If we could assign to it a cosmological explanation of the universe (which it does not have) we could compare it to 'Abdu'l-Bahá's 'voluntary formation' of existence described in Chapter Two.

In existentialism cause and effect are relegated to individual choices and their probabilities. The only reality it recognizes is the fact of existence itself wherein the individual discovers himself to be a free agent, free to act as he chooses, responsible only to and for himself. The power of choice reveals itself as acts of intentionality. Meaning and purpose have no significance outside of what the individual subjectively assigns to them.

In the attempt to bridge the Cartesian split between mind and matter, or subject and object, consciousness is defined as 'what we are conscious of'. Put another way, things exist so that existence can become conscious of itself. Reality and truth have no objectivity but exist as each individual's own inner composition. All being/matter is experienced as a kind of moment-to-moment, dimensionless, ever-present now which encompasses all phenomena. Reality and subjective consciousness are one.

Existentialism gives us a reality constituted by our own subjective probabilities, but seems to go no further; there is no acknowledgement of an objective reality apart from the subjective experience. Physical and natural laws seem to have been dismissed along with their inductive and empirical applications by science. It creates a strange, almost nihilistic world of a self-conscious reality with no cause-and-effect contingencies.

Language Philosophy

Language philosophy arose primarily to counteract the 'logical positivism' found in both philosophy and science by Ludwig Wittgenstein earlier in this century. The logical positivistic school insisted that meaning was conveyed by the logic of language, including mathematics, communicating the reality of the 'world-out-there' which could be verified by other linguistic propositions. Wittgenstein shook Western philosophy by proposing instead that the grammar of language and symbols contains no intrinsic meaning whatsoever, but that we create reality after the fact by how we learn to use words to fit specific cases. We impart sense to our language in the same way we learn to apply the correct rules for playing games. Games have no intrinsic meaning – we give them meaning by the rules we invent; but their meaning will have validity only if we apply their rules correctly.

For example, if two students have been instructed in algebra, and one student passes an exam by getting his answers right while the other one fails, it does not mean that one 'understood' the problems and that the other one did not. To do so would mean that equations have a built-in inherent universal meaning, which, of course, they do not. What has happened, says Wittgenstein, is that one student correctly learned the rules for applying algebraic symbols while the other one did not. Importantly, it is the way the rule is applied that determines its meaning. What we call reality is therefore meaningless; meaning is what we make it.

Wittgenstein's iconoclastic philosophy also attempts to destroy any comfort we may take in assuming we have an inner or private 'language' based on unconscious thought processes. He insisted that all our inner and outer responses are preceded by nothing more than our already having learned each circumstance or case established by others that allows us to make the proper choices and actions in life.

B (correct application of language) yields C (all reality); B not only explains C, it is C! The weakest part of his philosophy is the lack of an accounting for why and how the necessary abstract invention of language (A) to explain each case (B) could have arisen spontaneously in all civilizations precedent to its own conceptualization in the first place. That is, how could the original creative act of language have preceded the thought of it when there was no case or rule governing it?

Wittgenstein does not explain how any act of originality or creativity, including his own very original and creative philosophy, can take place in the absence of a prior case to work from. It is true that there are cases and circumstances which *resemble* them. But how does the creative person bridge that gap of resemblance, or even know that such a gap exists, unless an unconscious mental image peculiar only to him is envisioned and which sparks an intelligible bridge between this 'hidden language' and the language he has learned?

The language-is-everything premise abjures the traditional arguments of the older philosophies. It reduces the miracle of human consciousness to memorization exercises. It would seem that Wittgenstein has provided the ideal programme for creating artificial intelligence in the perfect computer – ourselves.

Behavioural Philosophy

At yet another extreme, behavioural philosophy reduces man to his physiological functions and the responses of others to them. As its name suggests, it borrows the stimulus/response framework of behavioural psychology, as well as drawing from both language philosophy and the existential concept of 'intentionality'. Trying to make them all compatible has resulted in basic propositions arguable more by what they omit than by what they tell us.

Emotions, for example, are not unconscious inner states, but are behavioural signals interpreted by others through our descriptions of them. We all learn how to send and receive these signals correctly in the same manner that we learn the rules of a game and correspondingly make our 'moves'. There is no place for insight, intuition, feelings, or other abstractions meant to describe inner states. Such explanations also attempt to rid us of that pesky Cartesian mind-body split by proposing that all life can be reduced to its basic physiological functions. We are told that all behaviour is learned by observing and memorizing the criteria which govern each act. This reduces all human behaviour to observable physical acts and their direct consequences.

The behavioural conclusion is exactly the opposite of the individual as free agent found in existentialism. Philosophically, its cosmological explanation of existence would fit 'Abdu'l-Bahá's 'involuntary formation' description of creation. Its attempt to explain all things in terms of observable behavioural acts of intention becomes so sparse that one can easily substitute 'primitive organism' or, as other critics have suggested, 'automaton' for 'human being' in all its examples.

The Way to Convergence

The above philosophies reduce existence to a 'nothing but' universe to explain *all* facets of life rather than *some* facets of life. Looking for the smallest constituent or the most basic concept to explain the totality of existence utilizes the fallacious logic of generalizing from the parts to the whole. This argument provides a constantly narrowing and restricting view of reality, leaving us with only the barest essentials. The basic message of the reductionists seems to be that traditional philosophy overlooked the obvious in its attempt to explain what was not.

Reductionists also dispense with grand theories and abstract models; there are no universals in their universes. God and the idea of an Absolute are considered to be religious inventions and, at worst, simplistic explanations for existence.

But without those grand theories and abstract models or the acceptance of universals, the reductionists have no way of gauging the accuracy of their own relativistic axioms. They all seem to be looking at life through the large end of the telescope. Their arenas have become so narrowly focused that they no longer have anything new to say. To their credit, they force us to examine our own ideological icons of 'how things are' and to challenge our cherished beliefs.

Philosophy stands somewhere between religion and theoretical science. If it is to revitalize itself, a good beginning might be to enlarge its focus for examining what it is possible to know. It can draw once again upon the continuing accumulation of truth-statements of science and religion and apply them to rethink man's conscious and unconscious responses to existence, to society and to himself. Only by reconsidering man's place in the larger universe can philosophy revitalize its search for truth and extend its boundaries into the hidden and unknown places of knowledge. A new philosophical model would at last converge to share the same paradigm of truth with theoretical science and divine revelation.

Probability and Predictability

Many of the continuing problems of philosophers and scientists result from their having failed truly to resolve the apparent dichotomy between subject and object, or mind and matter. This failure results in science's separation of probability (quantum mechanics) from predictability (Newtonian mechanics). In philosophy this problem revolves around whether to consider the individual as a free agent with free choice, or one who is acted upon (determinism) from the outside. The Bahá'í religion sees this as a spiritual question requiring a spiritual answer. In fact, a plausible explanation might even result in a common ground for all three disciplines.

We begin by merging the Bahá'í and GST models, both of which tell us that the smaller and more complex the system or component becomes, the more specialized it becomes, resulting in increasingly indeterminate behaviour with a decrease in the inclusiveness of its environment. We know that in the smallest of all worlds, the world of high-energy particles, traditional explanations do not account for their behaviour. On this level we can only know the *probable* behaviour of any single particle. All behaviour and motion seem to be chaotic – or perhaps not. There has been experimental evidence to show that even individual particles 'choose', in a most unpredictable fashion, to go where they want to go! When particles are beamed identically through a pinhole at a screen, each one strikes it at a different place, avoiding already targeted space. Our conclusion is that probable behaviour is not the same thing as chaotic or accidental behaviour. But if free choice can be equated with probability, and determinate behaviour with predictability, this raises some interesting interpretations for all the physical, social and behavioural sciences, as well as for religious philosophy.

At the other end of this view, the larger and more inclusive the system becomes, the easier it will be to make generalized statements and predictions about it. Once we learn the laws and principles that control it, whether we are speaking of galaxies or nations or political parties, the more accurate both our generalized assumptions and predictions will be concerning them. What we will not be able to generalize or predict are the actions of their individual components. For example, the commander of an army can predict the movements of his regiments but he cannot predict what a single infantryman will do. As for the beamed particles, the physicist cannot predict the point of impact for any single one but only how they will be generally distributed.

We can conclude that as a system moves outward towards inclusivity the fewer but more immutable will be the laws that govern it. As a result, the choices of its individual members will become more restricted as they become more bound to the larger laws of that system. This ensures the survival of the many over any one of its members and the triumph of the larger truth or law over the smaller. With this script, it is the hierarchy or system that controls and governs.

We see this ubiquitous principle at work everywhere in our daily lives, from bureaucratic pyramid-like organizations to the family unit where the individual wills of the children are subservient to the wills of their parents, the designers of each family system. Another example are the laws and ordinances on the city and regional levels, too numerous either to know or remember, to the fewer but more inclusive and far-reaching laws enacted by a national government.

Free Choice versus Determinism

The free choice versus determinism debate has been a preoccupation primarily of Western thought, having originated in the religion of Zoroastrianism some three thousand years ago. From there it entered Judaic and Greek philosophy, as well as other near eastern religions and cults, eventually finding its way into Christianity and Islam as a theological concept. Our definitions of these words are thus more religious than classically philosophical.

'Free will' relates to how free God has created man to exercise his own will in relation to God's Will. As we shall see, free will is more restrictive than 'free choice' which can be defined as unhindered action based upon individual decisions or desires.

'Determinism' refers to acts that will take place whether we have freely chosen them or not. These actions and events are seemingly 'determined' by forces set in motion outside us which we cannot control. In the past they were attributed to providence or fate. Now we speak of 'economic determinism', 'cultural determinism', and many other abstract 'determinisms'. They all tend to limit severely our ability to choose freely. Are we again confronted with a case of 'either-or'? How does free will or free choice fit into a world whose forces apparently overpower us? The Bahá'í teachings connect these various and often conflicting ideas into one unified spiritual concept.

For a Bahá'í, any fundamental explanation of human actions must be looked at on two levels; first, as an idea relating to what is conditioned or relative, and second, as an idea relating to what is unconditioned or Absolute. Put another way, one level has human definition and reality, and the other has Divine definition and Reality. In the religious sense, all finite possibilities are conditioned by what Divine Law has ordained. It is easy

157

to confuse the human with the Divine and mix metaphors as well as concepts, so to speak.

Western civilization traditionally sees this conflict as a contest between opposed ways of life when in fact free choice and determined action are one continuum, much like the positive/ negative scale describing human qualities and emotions discussed in Chapter Six. In this world of relative values we move back and forth from one side to the other exercising our alternatives (free choice) even as we submit to the authority of others (determinism). On the political level, one extreme results in tyranny and the other in anarchy. Perhaps good government exists when rulers know what and how to balance individual choices and when and how to limit and control group action.

For example, if there were no authority to which we could submit, we could not learn how to make intelligent choices; and if we did not learn to make intelligent choices, we could never learn how to let others govern us intelligently. Extending this example, if nature had not exerted her laws over us, we would still be struggling for species superiority. If God had not predetermined our evolutionary ascendancy, our species would now be extinct. Free choice and determinism are not in conflict; only our points of view concerning them and our definitions of them are.

If each one of us sat down tomorrow with a pencil and paper and made a list of all the choices we freely made over a twenty-four hour period, we might be startled and dismayed to discover that most of our actions and decisions are largely determined for us, if not by others, then by habit or tradition! Even hermits do not live completely by the rules of anarchy and chance. We come to realize that choices really consist of particular and accepted limited alternatives and options, like what to order for dinner on a pre-selected menu. Still, so long as we are free to make selections from these alternatives and options, satisfying our craving for novelty and excitement, the chance encounter or a new friendship, fulfilling challenges and changes, etc., we are content. At the same time, we prefer that someone else define our larger boundaries and give us the laws and rules that will order our social interactions and allow for material progress. As human beings, we seek a balance in all things, even in our choices. Without well-defined boundaries, free choice becomes licence; our inner and outer security and comfort depend upon acceptable boundaries.

If we could define determinism as an absolute, it would be a way of looking at undifferentiation, or the Divine Unity. In the greater world of God there is no split between independent action and determined action, so the issue itself is moot. In the realm of the Absolute there is no individual free will but only the Will of God. The problematic nature of this issue has importance only in this life. True determinism is what God has mandated through His Laws for His creation.

In the book *Some Answered Questions* a chapter is devoted to the discussion of free will versus determinism. 'Abdu'l-Bahá states clearly that only in matters of choosing between good and evil does man exercise his free will. This matter of choice devolves upon man as a decree from God, that is, it is predetermined, so that every individual must choose either a path to illumination and perfection or to ignorance and degradation. Only in these matters is he a free agent. Even this statement has within it a strange paradox that, if contemplated, is the key to solving it. This positive/negative split forever removed undifferentiation from the levels of relative existence, causing us to choose between ignorance (evil) or illumination (good). Only in the life to come, in the realm of oneness, does it recapture its original condition of completeness and perfection, where the active/positive and passive/negative forces operate as *one* power.

Glimpses into the nature of highly spiritualized individuals indicate that they have resolved the problem of choosing between good and evil actions. The personages we know as the Holy Manifestations of God, occupying both a divine and a human station, possess all the virtues and have perfect knowledge; They do not make wrong choices. 'Abdu'l-Bahá, representing the perfect example of the purely human condition, often made choices on behalf of others. In His own life situation, He knew what constituted right decision and action.

The closer to completeness and perfection we come in this life, the closer to the Absolute we are, our need to make choices diminishes in proportion. That is, wrong choices force us to make *more* choices. Potentially, in this life we are the fulfilment of this interchangeable power between positive and negative, active and passive. Our test of wisdom seems to be how well we utilize this power even as we recognize our captivity to God's Will.

Arguments from Design, Cause and Purpose

To seek, to know, to act. How much these words encompass when they are applied to our inner development, and how difficult to accomplish. When we shift them to apply to a course of action for reaching humankind as a whole, they seem even more remote and impossible to apply. How can the thoughts, feelings or actions of any one person affect the collective whole? If left to our own solutions it is not likely that we would ever successfully leave square one – good intentions – and move to square two – acting upon them. To do so involves a resolve of both will and purpose. That is, the exercising of volition in the one instant and something we call 'purpose' in the second.

The teleological explanation for a universe with purpose (predetermined causation) has been almost completely erased from both scientific and philosophical literature, along with a first, last or any cause. The reason is an obvious one – God as Creator (First Cause) would become science's 'final' equation and philosophy's ultimate proposition. Neither discipline publicly accepts such an accounting which would, apparently, forever stifle any further creative thinking or discoveries in their fields. In concrete matters of inductive applications, however, cause and effect are still very much a part of our scientific technologies.

A belief in origination with purpose through an ultimate but unknowable Intelligence has been held by a majority of the world's most profound thinkers, a belief that does not appear to have suppressed or stifled their creative thought processes. An omniscient God surely delights in human brilliance and creativity and rejoices in our successes in unlocking the secrets of our universe, an infinite endeavour which, the Bahá'í Faith assures us, is the purpose and goal of intelligent life everywhere.

The 'argument from design', or a master plan of cause and effect from which nothing can deviate, is not quite the same as the teleological argument. It was the product of Western Judaic-Christian theological thought reinforced by both Islam and the Greco-Ptolemaic universe which remained unchallenged until the seventeenth century. Even though Copernicus changed humanity's view of the cosmos, the 'new science' and accompanying philosophies of scepticism could not destroy the underlying belief in God as original causation. The explanations of Bahá'u'lláh and 'Abdu'l-Bahá of the existence of God utilize

160

both the theological and 'argument from design' premises, but in a new format.

The Bahá'í teachings subscribe to creation as process with the possibility that many material universes may have come and gone, all different, exhibiting not chance as cause and effect, but God as an eternal Creator of an infinite transformational universe based on His Laws. God's 'plans' would not only vary, but would exhibit both probability and destination, as our own universe and existence show. The Bahá'í religion, like GST, allows for destination for the larger cases and categories, and probability for the smaller, more specialized cases and categories. Western thought is still locked in its ancient prison of a limited either/or universe, long obsolete. If we plug in the more enlightened idea of guided probability, it explains how each creation has been designed with powerful physical and spiritual laws which may produce different outcomes. Nonetheless, each and every cosmic possibility will reflect God's wisdom, His love, His justice and His mercies and bounties, each of which are themselves capable of an infinite variety of expressions. Throughout His creational processes, He remains the Originating Principle, the First and Last Cause, the Fashioner and Designer of infinite 'plans'.

The Meaning of Purpose

The various branches of science continue to restrict themselves to this same obsolete either/or universe by their reluctance to attribute original causation to an unknown Intelligence. Nonetheless, they remain vitally concerned with the *effects* this non-existent cause has produced. Somehow, *purpose* continues to lurk in the background along with *meaning* to haunt them. Any causal explanation of any phenomenon (effect) immediately opens the door to its meaning. It is not difficult to take the next step and surmise that what has meaning very likely has purpose, two issues that some scientists try to avoid by substituting 'function' for purpose, and relegating 'meaning' to information or data. Others have realized that the quest for information is not the same as the quest for knowledge and wisdom.

Still, it is science that pulls out from reality the mechanics of the universe, but it is revelatory truth that provides its housing.

The traditional role of philosophy has been to speculate on the ramifications offered by both. Any contradictions that exist between reason and spirit have been artificially created by us. The universe is reasonable and life is reasonable, and it is the human spirit which directs our reason to wonder why this is so. It is difficult not to conclude that the explanatory power of *meaning* is the same as the explanatory power of *purpose*. Consciousness, thought and awareness are all ingredients of the rational order of mind – the human spirit – whose purpose it is to understand.

Synthesis

The Bahá'í religion puts the individual's and society's search for meaning and purpose in an expanded perspective. It supplies a comprehensive synthesis for bringing about a new cycle of human progress and endeavour. It is not the 'converting' to a new religion that Bahá'u'lláh sought to accomplish, but the providing of means to bring about the Golden Age of humanity. Without the motivation of purpose to give meaning and usefulness to our experiences of life, we are bereft of hope and happiness. Without the purposeful meaning and usefulness of life, civilizations, with their arts and sciences, could not have been built. It is strange to think that while believers in an atheistic philosophy admit to a 'purpose' for their own particular work and individual lives, they do not assign any to the generality of existence.

> God's purpose in sending His Prophets unto men is twofold. The first is to liberate the children of men from the darkness of ignorance, and guide them to the light of true understanding. The second is to ensure the peace and tranquillity of mankind, and provide all the means by which they can be established.[5]

> What must be the result of a human life? It is evident that the goal is not to eat, sleep, dress and repose on the couch of negligence. No, it is to find one's way to reality, and understand the divine signs; to receive wisdom from the Lord of Lords, and to move steadily forward like a great sea.[6]

These two statements about the purpose of life – one by Bahá'u'lláh and the other by 'Abdu'l-Bahá – make it clear that the reality which gives purpose and meaning to all of our other realities is a spiritual one. As individuals we are free either to deny and reject this proposition or to accept and act upon it. What we are not free to do is to refuse to make this choice.

11

Conclusion

Each chapter in this book has been written with a particular logical and sequential unfoldment of spiritual truth. That is, each succeeding chapter is most easily understood after having mastered the ideas in the preceding ones. Each subject is treated as a separate path to truth. As the reader approached the end of the book, he will have realized that truth, knowledge, perfection, love, will, etc., are all descriptive nouns describing the same thing – reality – and that this collection of the real is but a mirror image of God's Truth, Knowledge, Perfection, Love, Will, etc., all describing the Divine Reality. We at last understand that this one point of unity truly encompasses all realities; it is both the beginning and the end, the First Cause as well as the Last Cause.

Chapter One, including the fable of the Circadians, in a curious way, is also Chapter Ten, as well as providing the themes for all the chapters in between. There would be no single point of truth if it could not somehow be pictured or interpreted. The point becomes the circling word. In the world of relativities, truth, like the primordial atom, ends where it began. This idea was also eloquently conveyed by T.S. Eliot in his last poetic masterpiece, 'Four Quartets', in the first five and last lines of the last stanza of this work:

> We shall not cease from exploration
> And the end of all our exploring
> Will be to arrive where we started
> And know the place for the first time.
> Through the unknown, remembered gate . . .
> And the fire and the rose are one.[1]

CONCLUSION

The Bahá'í religion also completes a circle. It offers the world the first unified model of the universe with an explanation all humanity is capable of comprehending. If its guidance to mankind is to last, each individual should be able, on his own, to understand his true nature and the role he must play in bringing about a unified world. Achieving the goal of world peace, for example, should no longer remain the dream of idealists; it should now be seen as an urgent mandate from God for all people and all nations. The religious, racial and political unity of this planet should be seen as a corollary, or perhaps the result, of the goal of a lasting world peace.

Every individual has been given the inner and outer resources to realize his full potentialities, a goal which both Bahá'u'lláh and 'Abdu'l-Bahá said was the purpose of each life and the basis for all inward and outward change in the world. But without a new spiritual system to bring about a new social order that will uphold and maintain every individual's and every nation's rights and dignity, there will be no incentive for people and governments to change. The mission of Bahá'u'lláh is to bring this about.

Followers of the Bahá'í Faith believe their religion has ushered in a New Age based on this new socio-spiritual model, which has resulted in the dramatic changes already taking place in our world and which is re-ordering our lives and the governments of the nations we populate. Bahá'ís argue that traditional explanations are no longer capable of showing us the overall design or pretending that no such design exists. Humanity has suffered its 'rites of passage' and has come of age.

No longer is it individuals, acting alone, who must accept responsibility for our actions; it is now mankind as a whole which is answerable to God.

When no one was looking, it seems a new heaven and a new earth were being set in place. Now all of us must take care of them and see to it that they flourish. Perhaps in a distant future travellers from another remote galaxy will stop by our planet to exchange versions of truth and reality with us. Our legacy to our progeny should not disappoint – in our own starry galaxy it may be that we will be known as 'ancient homo sapiens sapiens', the old and very wise people of the planet Earth.

References

Introduction

1. Ford, Mary Hanley, 'With 'Abdu'l-Bahá in Paris', *Star of the West*, vol. 2, no. 14 (23 November 1911), p. 14.

Chapter 1: Escape to Reality

1. 'Abdu'l-Bahá, *Promulgation*, p. 270.
2. ibid. p. 14.
3. ibid. p. 21.
4. ibid. pp. 49–50.
5. ibid. pp. 60–1.
6. ibid. pp. 326–7.
7. Barney, Laura Clifford, 'Only a Word', *Bahá'í World*, vol. 5, p. 667.
8. 'Abdu'l-Bahá, 'Tablet to Dr Auguste Forel', *Star of the West*, vol. 14, no. 4 (July 1923), pp. 103–7. See also Mühlschlegel, Peter, *Auguste Forel and the Bahá'í Faith*. Oxford: George Ronald, 1978.

Chapter 2: The Originating Principle and Beyond

1. Bahá'u'lláh, *Gleanings*, p. 48.
2. ibid. pp. 62–3.
3. 'Abdu'l-Bahá, *Foundations*, p. 53.
4. 'Abdu'l-Bahá, *Selections*, p. 53.
5. *Star of the West*, vol. 3, no. 14 (23 November 1912), p. 9n.
6. See *Promulgation*, pp. 421–5 and *Star of the West*, vol. 6, no. 33 (28 April 1915), p. 22.
7. 'Abdu'l-Bahá, *Promulgation*, p. 421.
8. *Star of the West*, vol. 6, no. 3 (28 April 1915), p. 22.
9. ibid. p. 23.

10. ibid. p. 24.
11. Bahá'u'lláh, *Prayers and Meditations*, pp. 48–9.
12. ibid. p. 49.
13. ibid. p. 222.
14. 'Abdu'l-Bahá, *Foundations*, pp. 52–3.
15. 'Abdu'l-Bahá, *Some Answered Questions*, p. 203.
16. 'Abdu'l-Bahá, *Divine Philosophy*, pp. 76–7.
17. Bahá'u'lláh, *Gleanings*, p. 61.
18. 'Abdu'l-Bahá, *Some Answered Questions*, p. 203.
19. Bahá'u'lláh, *Hidden Words*, Arabic, nos. 3, 4 and 64.
20. 'Abdu'l-Bahá, *Some Answered Questions*, pp. 158–9.

Chapter 3: The Worlds of God

1. Bahá'u'lláh, *Tablets*, pp. 140–2.
2. 'Abdu'l-Bahá, *Some Answered Questions*, pp. 293–4.
3. ibid. pp. 205–6.
4. 'Abdu'l-Bahá, *Promulgation*, p. 58.
5. 'Abdu'l-Bahá, *Foundations*, p. 58.
6. 'Abdu'l-Bahá, *Paris Talks*, p. 59.
7. *Reality of Man*, pp. 43–4.

Chapter 4: The Journey of the Atom

1. *Reality of Man*, p. 21.
2. 'Abdu'l-Bahá, *Foundations*, pp. 57 and 58.
3. The First Law of Thermodynamics states that energy can neither be created nor destroyed. The Third Law states that the total amount of energy in the universe, including its mass equivalent, remains constant.
4. 'Abdu'l-Bahá, *Promulgation*, pp. 302–3.
5. 'Abdu'l-Bahá, *Some Answered Questions*, p. 192.
6. 'Abdu'l-Bahá, *Paris Talks*, pp. 96–7.

Chapter 5: The Soul by Any Other Name

1. 'Abdu'l-Bahá, *Some Answered Questions*, pp. 235–6.
2. ibid. p. 239–40.
3. Bahá'u'lláh, *Epistle*, p. 112.
4. Bahá'u'lláh, *Gleanings*, pp. 161–2.
5. 'Abdu'l-Bahá, *Divine Philosophy*, p. 98.
6. *Reality of Man*, p. 26.

7. Bahá'u'lláh, *Gleanings*, p. 164.
8. Bahá'u'lláh, 'Tablet to Ra'is', *Star of the West*, vol. 14, no. 1 (April 1923), p. 8.
9. *Bahá'í Revelation*, pp. 229–30.
10. *Star of the West*, vol. 14, no. 1 (April 1923), p. 11.
11. 'Abdu'l-Bahá, *Promulgation*, p. 418.
12. 'Abdu'l-Bahá, *Selections*, p. 190.
13. *Star of the West*, vol. 7, no. 19 (2 March 1917), p. 190.
14. 'Abdu'l-Bahá, *Paris Talks*, p. 97.
15. ibid. pp. 97–8.
16. ibid. pp. 98–9.
17. 'Abdu'l-Bahá, *Some Answered Questions*, pp. 236–7.

Chapter 6: The Paradoxical Nature of the Unity of Opposites

1. 'Abdu'l-Bahá, *Promulgation*, pp. 294–6.
2. 'Abdu'l-Bahá, *Some Answered Questions*, p. 263.
3. Cobb, *Character*, p. 73.
4. Bahá'u'lláh, *Gleanings*, p. 149.
5. Esslemont, J.E., 'Religion and Science in the Light of the Bahá'í Revelation', *Star of the West*, vol. 8, no. 7 (13 July 1917), p. 75.
6. 'Abdu'l-Bahá, *Some Answered Questions*, p. 216.
7. ibid. p. 123.
8. ibid. p. 126.
9. ibid. p. 264.
10. 'Abdu'l-Bahá, *Promulgation*, p. 465.
11. *Star of the West*, vol. 10, no. 7 (13 July 1919), pp. 126–7.
12. Holley, Horace, 'The Spiritual Basis of World Peace', *Bahá'í World*, vol. V, p. 517.

Chapter 7: Knowledge and Perfection: Little by Little, Degree by Degree

1. 'Abdu'l-Bahá, *Promulgation*, pp. 304–5.
2. 'Abdu'l-Bahá, *Divine Philosophy*, p. 73.
3. 'Abdu'l-Bahá, *Promulgation*, p. 21.
4. ibid.
5. ibid. p. 22.
6. ibid.
7. Bahá'u'lláh, *Seven Valleys*, p. 12.
8. ibid. p. 15.

9. 'Abdu'l-Bahá, *Promulgation*, p. 303.
10. 'Abdu'l-Bahá, *Some Answered Questions*, p. 177.
11. ibid. pp. 178–9.
12. Morten, Marjory, 'The Passing of Bahíyyih Khánum, *Bahá'í World*, vol. V, p. 185.
13. 'Abdu'l-Bahá, *Divine Philosophy*, pp. 80–1.
14. ibid. p. 81.
15. 'Abdu'l-Bahá, *Some Answered Questions*, p. 230.

Chapter 8: The Universal Glue

1. Baha'u'lláh, *Hidden Words*, Arabic, nos. 3, 4, 5, 7, 9 and 19.
2. *Bahá'í World*, vol. IV, p. 500.
3. 'Abdu'l-Bahá, *Selections*, p. 27.
4. 'Abdu'l-Bahá, *Foundations*, pp. 88–9.
5. 'Abdu'l-Bahá, *Divine Philosophy*, p. 82.
6. 'Abdu'l-Bahá, *Foundations*, p. 83.
7. 'Abdu'l-Bahá, *Paris Talks*, p. 180.
8. ibid. p. 181.
9. *Divine Art of Living*, p. 115.
10. *Star of the West*, vol. 8, no. 10 (8 September 1917), p. 134.
11. ibid., vol. 8, no. 11 (27 September 1917), p. 139.
12. ibid. p. 121.
13. Bahá'u'lláh, *Seven Valleys*, p. 8.
14. ibid.
15. Bahá'u'lláh, *Hidden Words*, Persian, no. 40.
16. Bahá'u'lláh, *Seven Valleys*, pp. 9–11.
17. *Diary of Juliet Thompson*, p. xv.
18. ibid. p. 6.
19. ibid. pp. 9–10.
20. ibid. p. 18.
21. ibid. pp. 33–4.
22. ibid. p. 37.
23. ibid. pp. 82–3.

Chapter 9: If Life Follows Death, Where is Time?

1. 'Abdu'l-Bahá, *Selections*, p. 204.
2. ibid. p. 177.
3. Bahá'u'lláh, *Gleanings*, p. 157.
4. *Reality of Man*, p. 32.
5. 'Abdu'l-Bahá, *Divine Philosophy*, p. 76.

6. 'Abdu'l-Bahá, *Paris Talks*, p. 93.
7. *Reality of Man*, pp. 29–31.
8. Bahá'u'lláh, *Seven Valleys*, p. 25.
9. 'Abdu'l-Bahá, *Paris Talks*, p. 66.
10. Qur'án, Sura 57.
11. Revelation 22:13.
12. Bahá'u'lláh, *Gleanings*, p. 54.
13. Bahá'u'lláh, *Seven Valleys*, pp. 26–7.
14. ibid. p. 28.
15. 'Abdu'l-Bahá, *Some Answered Questions*, p. 229.
16. Bahá'u'lláh, *Gleanings*, p. 153.
17. ibid. p. 156.
18. ibid. p. 154.
19. ibid. pp. 155–6.
20. ibid. p. 155.

Chapter 10: Resurgence, Convergence and Synthesis

1. 'Abdu'l-Bahá, *Selections*, p. 69.
2. ibid. pp. 68–9.
3. ibid. p. 69.
4. Bahá'u'lláh, *Gleanings*, p. 136.
5. ibid. pp. 79–80.
6. 'Abdu'l-Bahá, *Divine Philosophy*, p. 26.

Chapter 11: Conclusion

1. Eliot, *Four Quartets*.

Bibliography

'Abdu'l-Bahá. *'Abdu'l-Bahá on Divine Philosophy*. Compiled by Isabel Fraser-Chamberlain. Boston, Mass.: The Tudor Press, 1916.

—— *Foundations of World Unity*. Wilmette, Illinois: Bahá'í Publishing Trust, 1955.

—— *Paris Talks*. London: Bahá'í Publishing Trust, 1961.

—— *The Promulgation of Universal Peace*. Compiled by Howard MacNutt. Wilmette, Illinois: Bahá'í Publishing Trust, 2nd ed. 1982.

—— *Selections from the Writings of 'Abdu'l-Bahá*. Translated by a Committee at the Bahá'í World Centre and by Marzieh Gail. Haifa: Bahá'í World Centre, 1978.

—— *Some Answered Questions*. Collected and Translated from the Persian by Laura Clifford Barney. Wilmette, Illinois: Bahá'í Publishing Trust, rev. ed. 1981.

Bahá'í Revelation, The. A Selection from the Bahá'í Holy Writings. London: Bahá'í Publishing Trust, 1955.

Bahá'í World, The. vols. IV and V. Reprinted. Wilmette, Illinois: Bahá'í Publishing Trust, 1980.

Bahá'u'lláh. *Epistle to the Son of the Wolf*. Wilmette, Illinois: Bahá'í Publishing Trust, 1962.

—— *Gleanings from the Writings of Bahá'u'lláh*. Wilmette, Illinois: Bahá'í Publishing Trust, 1963.

—— *The Hidden Words of Bahá'u'lláh*. Wilmette, Illinois: Bahá'í Publishing Trust, 1954.

—— *Prayers and Meditations*. Wilmette, Illinois: Bahá'í Publishing Trust, 1979.

—— *The Seven Valleys and the Four Valleys*. Translated by Marzieh Gail (with Ali-Kuli Khan). Wilmette, Illinois: Bahá'í Publishing Trust, rev. ed. 1978.

—— *Tablets of Bahá'u'lláh revealed after the Kitáb-i-Aqdas*. Com-

171

piled by the Research Department of the Universal House of Justice and translated by Habib Taherzadeh with the assistance of a Committee at the Bahá'í World Centre. Haifa: Bahá'í World Centre, 1978.

von Bertalanffy, Ludwig. *General System Theory*. New York: George Braziller, 1968.

Cobb, Stanwood. *Character: A Spiritual Sequence in Psychology*. Washington: The Avalon Press, 1938.

Diary of Juliet Thompson, The. Los Angeles, Calif.: Kalimat Press, 1983.

Divine Art of Living, The. Compiled by Mabel Hyde Paine. Wilmette, Illinois: Bahá'í Publishing Committee, 1944.

Eliot, T.S. *Four Quartets*. New York: Harcourt, Brace and World, Inc., 1971.

Jantsch, Erich. *Design for Evolution*. New York: George Braziller, 1975.

Laszlo, Ervin. *A Systems View of the World*. New York: George Braziller, 1972.

Reality of Man, The. Excerpts from the Writings of Bahá'u'lláh and 'Abdu'l-Bahá. Wilmette, Illinois: Bahá'í Publishing Trust, 1966.

Star of the West. Reprinted. Oxford: George Ronald, 1984.

Sutherland, John W. *A General Systems Philosophy for the Social and Behavioral Sciences*. New York: George Braziller, 1973.

Logic and Logos

Essays on Science, Religion and Philosophy

by WILLIAM S. HATCHER

Five astute essays linking modern mathematics and logic with issues traditionally the concern of philosophy and theology:

Platonism and Pragmatism

Myths, Models and Mysticism

From Metaphysics to Logic

A Logical Solution to the Problem of Evil

Science and the Bahá'í Faith

Professor of Mathematics in the Faculty of Sciences and Engineering at Laval University, Hatcher explores the interface between disciplines now approaching each other at last after centures of mutual mistrust.

160 pages
Softcover only, £4.50, US$9.50, Can$10.50   ISBN 0–85398–298–8

The Eternal Quest for God

An Introduction to the Divine Philosophy of 'Abdu'l-Bahá

by JULIO SAVI

'Throughout the universe on the traces of God'

What can we know of God? How can evolution be explained? What is the nature of the human soul?

Julio Savi ranges over the whole field of Bahá'í sacred text to explore the deepest questions of existence. As the translator into Italian of most of the major Bahá'í texts published in the last twenty years, Savi was eminently qualified to undertake the meticulous research required to produce this far-reaching and profound examination of the philosophical concepts found in the Bahá'í religion.

288 pages
Softcover only, £8.50, US$15.95, Can$19.50   ISBN 0–85398–295–3

The Revelation of Bahá'u'lláh

by ADIB TAHERZADEH

A four-volume classic work describing Bahá'u'lláh's major works and a great number of Tablets as yet untranslated into English. Adib Taherzadeh covers the whole period of Bahá'u'lláh's ministry, from its birth in the dungeon of the Síyáh-Chál to the final years of Bahá'u'lláh's life when he took up residence in the Mansion of Bahjí. He adds to his analysis much fascinating background by recounting events in the life of Bahá'u'lláh and in the lives of his companions and followers, enhanced by memoirs of the time and photographs.

1861 pages in four volumes, 101 illustrations   ISBN 0–85398–311–9
Softcover only, complete four-volume set with study guide, £38.00, US$75.00, Can$90.00

The Search for a Just Society
by John Huddleston

A masterly and comprehensive analysis of the impulse towards justice which drives human civilization forward. Huddleston considers:

* the role of religion – both western and eastern
* the role of three major revolutions, in England, America and France
* movements towards greater political and social equality: the abolition of slavery and serfdom, the emancipation of women, the establishment of democracy and the rule of law
* efforts to reduce material poverty: trade unions, socialism and the welfare state
* attempts to move from war to peace: the Congress System, the League of Nations, the United Nations

John Huddleston has been a senior staff member at the International Monetary Fund for more than a decade where he is presently Chief of the Planning and Budget Division and Assistant Director in the Administration Department.

528 pages, 29 tables, 3 maps, 12 pages of illustrations
Hardcover only, £19.95, US$39.95, Can$40.50

ISBN 0–85398–288–0

George Ronald, Publisher

George Ronald is best known as one of the leading publishers of books about the Bahá'í Faith. There are over 120 titles in our current catalogue, including sections on peace, global issues, racism, equality, family life, education, personal transformation, spirituality, prayer, philosophy, religion, art, poetry, children's books, biography, and academic and reference books.

George Ronald books are available from all good bookshops and libraries, or can be ordered direct. Just fill in the form below and list the titles you want.

NAME (block letters)

_____

ADDRESS

_____

_____

_____

☐ Tick this box if you would like a copy of our catalogue and price list.

Please send to George Ronald, Publisher, 46 High Street, Kidlington, Oxford OX5 2DN, England. Please enclose cheque, postal or money order to the value of the purchase price, plus postage and packing as follows:

Payment in sterling: Orders up to £25, add £1.00. Post free on orders over £25.

Payment in dollars: Orders up to $50 (US or Canadian), add $3.00. Post free on orders over $50.

While every effort is made to keep prices low, it is sometimes necessary to increase prices at short notice. George Ronald, Publisher reserve the right to show new retail prices on covers which may differ from those previously advertised in the text or elsewhere.